A GRAIN OF SAND

To my good friend Tom Kelly with best wishes

Fred Shelley

A GRAIN OF SAND

Fred Shelley

The Book Guild Ltd
Sussex, England

First published in Great Britain in 2003 by
The Book Guild Ltd,
25 High Street,
Lewes, East Sussex
BN7 2LU

Copyright © Fred Shelley 2003

The right of Fred Shelley to be identified as the author of this work has been asserted by him in accordance with the Copyright, Designs and Patents Act 1988.

All rights reserved. No part of this publication may be reproduced, transmitted, or stored in a retrieval system, in any form or by any means, without permission in writing from the publisher, nor be otherwise circulated in any form of binding or cover other than that in which it is published and without a similar condition being imposed on the subsequent purchaser.

Typesetting in Times by
IML Typographers, Birkenhead, Merseyside

Printed in Great Britain by
Bath Press Ltd, Bath

A catalogue record for this book is
available from The British Library

ISBN 1 85776 727 6

CONTENTS

Introduction		ix
1	Early Years	1
2	School	9
3	An Austin Apprentice; Girlfriends	16
4	Sports and Courtship	29
5	Marriage and War	37
6	Mansfield	46
7	Bristol	53
8	King's Heath Engineering – Beginnings	63
9	Industrial Relations and Machines	82
10	Caravans and Boats	91
11	King's Heath Engineering – Expansion	97
12	Boat Trips Abroad	108
13	Masonic Experiences	118
14	Ruin	120
15	North Wales and Retirement	124

A Grain of Sand

Consider the Sahara desert, many thousands of square miles of unknown depth; take the grains of sands therein as representing the lives of human beings since the beginning of time. Some grains are blown in sandstorms all over the world, some infiltrate clothes, tyres, vehicles, aircraft, animal hoofs and are taken on journeys, experiences and untold adventures. My autobiography is the story of one such 'Grain of Sand'.

A weather bulletin on 28th October, 1987 reported that a freak wind had caused grains of sand from the Sahara to fall in Wiltshire, England, and also in Norway.

On this date I started to write my story.

INTRODUCTION

How does one begin to write one's own life story? For me it's best to recall its most salient event and then branch off in a series of tangents, each one displaying a facet of life. To this end I must take you back to 1938.

I was 22 years of age, and working with the Austin Motor Company. I had just finished six years of study in mechanical and production engineering, coming second out of a total of 900 apprentices, and had been presented with a gold watch by Lord Austin. Because of my success as a trainee toolmaker I was nominated Austin Apprentice of the year and invited to attend a presentation ceremony at the Dorchester Hotel, London. The presentation was made by King George VI and Queen Elizabeth, and this was the first time I had ever mixed with royalty. My room at the Dorchester was paid for by the company.

I made the journey to and from London in a six-year-old Austin Seven that I had bought for £29 out of cash earned as a tea boy at Austin. On the return journey to Birmingham, disaster struck. The car broke down very near to a transport hostel on the main Whitney road. I had just managed to push the car to the car park when the driver of a massive lorry came over and said, 'What's the matter, son?' I didn't know. He immediately fetched his tools, lifted the bonnet and diagnosed the fault. 'The bevel gears of the drive of the distributor have stripped,' he said, 'leave it to me. I'll fix it, but let's have a meal first.' After many mugs of tea he arranged beds for the night. That night I lay thinking, What a strange world – one night a private room at the Dorchester Hotel, the next a dormitory with transport drivers.

After rising, a wash, and a transport breakfast, I asked the owner of the hostel the whereabouts of my new friend. 'He's driven off,' he said, 'but don't worry. He'll be back shortly.' Sure enough, half an hour later, he was. 'OK son, your car is ready.' He would not accept a penny piece; only a mug of tea. He had risen early, driven to Oxford in his massive lorry, picked up a pair of gears from a storekeeper friend who owed him a favour, driven back, and repaired the engine. As his firm paid for his time, accommodation and meals, he saw no reason to accept anything for helping a fellow human being. Truly, a knight of the road.

I returned to Birmingham full of gratitude and well-being. This was surely one of the highlights of my life, to be remembered and cherished as proof that man's humanity to man still exists.

1

Early Years

My grandfather (on Dad's side) was an inventor and worked for a small company, later taken over by Tube Investments. He designed and developed the first free-wheel cycle gear, and also the cow-catcher device fitted to early trains and trams. The first trams were horse-drawn and in crowded streets accidents were plentiful, caused by people falling under the unprotected wheels of vehicles. My grandfather's free-wheel cycle gear had locked teeth for forward drive but tapered ratchet teeth for free wheeling. My grandfather had three sons and a daughter.

My father, Alfred, was the eldest of his four children; his brother Len two years younger, his sister May three years younger and the youngest son, Chris, a further two years younger. My grandfather died at the age of 33, and left Alfred at nine years old as head of the family. Because of their circumstances, living in the slums of Gregore Street, my grandfather was buried in what was called a pauper's grave.

My father, at nine years of age in 1893, had to rise at 5.00 a.m., walk to Sir Harry's Road, perhaps a mile away, polish all the shoes at the house, return and deliver papers, before going to school. Eventually my grandmother remarried, a Mr Butler, and the family lived in Upper Emily Street, Highgate.

My mother, Edith Dixon, was the eldest daughter in a large

family of nine. She married my father on 30th August, 1914. At about that time my father was called up, and was waiting on Birmingham New Street Station with a friend, George Jennings, both in khaki, when they were withdrawn from the assembly to start in a factory at Longbridge, run by a Mr Austin, to build small transport cars for the army. These two friends were to become lifetime associates. George and his wife Lily had a daughter, Eileen, on 12th March, 1917. I was born 19th September, 1916. My brother and Eileen's sister both arrived four years later. My earliest recollection, at nearly four years old, is of thanking the doctor for the delivery of my brother Victor.

Our house in Dymoke Street was a two-bedroom terraced house on one side of an entry. My Auntie Vin had a converted drapery shop the other side of the entry. The entry widened out into a courtyard of five houses with an outside two-holer toilet at the far end. One of these houses housed my mother's brother and his family: Harold, one year younger than me, Roland, Thelma, Billy and Tom. We had a yard at the back of our house, paved in grey glazed bricks, a washhouse with a toilet at the back, and at the end of the yard an alcove to house the dustbin. This was called the miskin. One of my early memories is of my dad building a chicken run in the yard where six chickens were kept. Two further doors away was a button factory, Bells. My dad, a toolmaker, worked on tools for the factory in his spare time, to earn a little extra money.

During my early years I was a weakling and had every children's illness one after the other. Mother had an old treadle sewing machine on which she used to help her sister Vin make dresses for the shop, and clothes for us all. I remember I used to play for hours moving the treadle by its vertical rod, as it became a tram, a car, or a ship in my imagination. Another of my early pastimes was to shuffle in the dust of Highgate Park and pretend I was sliding in snow, or was a train. If ever I was missing this was where I would be found.

My favourite toys were four angle brackets, on which I stood screws which became Vikings or pirates enacting land and sea battles in my imagination.

There were two rival gangs of children in the district, Dymoke Street gang and Emily Street gang. The captain of the Emily Street gang was a strapping lad, Tony, about 15 or 16, built like Errol Flynn, good-looking, athletic and very good at sports. Rodney was the Dymoke Street captain. We played football in the street, with the goals the entries on either side of the street. We also played cricket with a lamp-post as wicket; more often than not the ball was made of old clothes tied with tape. Other games included rounders, tipcat, cock horse, and cops and robbers.

Tipcat consisted of batting a dolly, or tipcat, a small piece of wood about four inches long with each end tapered. The batting side had a turn each at striking the tapered end with a bat, and as the dolly rose in the air hitting it with the full force of the bat. Then a discussion between rival members began, to decide the number of strides between the base and where the dolly landed. Tony was a past master at covering the distance in the agreed number of strides. He always did the strides, hops and jumps for Emily Street and it amazed me the distance he could cover with his prowess. If the tipcat was caught before it touched the ground the whole batting side was out, and the fielders had their turn to bat. I fondly remember one of our games of tipcat on a Saturday morning, when my friend Jim's mother called for him just as he was about to bat. Someone shouted 'Come on in, Jim, your mother wants yer boots to go shopping.' This call was not unusual. The boys were supplied with boots from the council, while their mothers used to wear slippers constructed from herdan or hessian bags. When they went out they used the boys' boots, and the boys had to wear the slippers.

The game cock horse was played with two teams. The team playing horse had the captain standing at the head while his team-mates each bent from the waist with his head tucked into the lad's bottom in front. The other team took a run and each jumped on the horse as far forward as possible, to allow room for the rest of the team. The horse team had to withstand the weight of all the jumpers, and if ever they collapsed under the strain, the winning jumpers shouted, 'Weak horses! All my men on and off again.' The exercise was repeated until the horse team, by interchanging various members, were able to contain the jumpers to the count of ten. Then the roles were reversed.

Cops and robbers was another pastime. One end of the street was called the 'headquarters' and diagonally opposite was the 'police station'. The roadway was a deep, swift-flowing impassable river and anyone stepping off the pavement was drowned. The only place to cross the road was at a lamp-post, which denoted a bridge. The loot was a piece of wood or coal which had to be taken from the police station to headquarters by the robbers, and intercepted by the cops. Sometimes fierce struggles took place and there were always a few bloodied heads, knees and hands after that game. We also played marbles, and skimmers.

Marbles was played by drawing a chalk circle on the floor and marbles rolling so that they stayed inside the circle. An alley, tat or tatty was placed in the centre of the circle and players tried to just touch the tat and stay in the circle. If this was accomplished the successful competitor won two marbles off each of his opponents. The winner was the one with the most left. We all started with ten marbles each.

Skimmers were played with cigarette cards. One 'diddy' card was leaned against the wall and competitors took turns to try and skim another card to knock down the diddy. When this was accomplished the successful player collected all the

These regular travellers formed themselves into the 'Wayfarers' and met each week at the Kings Head, Alcester, to hold regular concerts. It was these meetings that helped my father decide to move to King's Heath.

As a family, we used to go on holiday to Bromsgrove with the Jenningses, whose two daughters were the same age as my brother and me. It was the dearest wish of our respective parents that one day the families would become united.

Both George Jennings and my father acquired motorcycle combinations and during the summer months used to exchange visits between Dymoke Street and Aston, where the Jenningses had a sweet shop. We all used to turn out together on a Sunday afternoon, with Mother and Vic in the sidecar and me as pillion, whilst Eileen rode pillion with her sister and her mother in their sidecar.

Whenever Grandma Dixon held a party the Jenningses attended. The evening was spent with songs around the piano, played by Mum's brother Sid. At times there were over 30 in one room round the piano.

I was always a good listener when Dad spoke of his job and his tribulations. He was a strong trade unionist when he first started at the Austin factory and always defended the working man. I used to listen to his tales of how the management persuaded him from being the workers' representative to promote him to foreman of the press tool room.

At the time of the General Strike in 1926 things were very bad. All trade unionists were on strike and management carried on working the machines, and on the bench. Dad came home every Friday with the same story: no cash for wages, but shares in the company in lieu. His share holdings reached about 2,000 shares. In his spare time he took up shoe repair, not only for the family but for the neighbours. He also made press tools for the button factory. Often after a day's work he worked right through the night to earn a few previous cards that had missed. A new diddy card was placed and the game continued.

During all our street games the housewives stood or sat outside their own front doors and watched, occasionally shouting instructions or derision.

Every week we would decide how to spend our Saturday pocket money of one penny each. We could spend a halfpenny on the weekly comic *Chips*, a farthing on chewing gum or gobstoppers, and a farthing on a variety of sweets. We used to exchange comics so we each had three to read per week. The gobstopper expenditure was a must. A gobstopper was a sweet about an inch in diameter and made of different colours. As each colour was sucked off another different colour appeared. The job was never to bite through but suck off each colour. The sweet lasted hours.

Another exercise we undertook was to deliver a cart of coal to various addresses. The rate was a farthing, but you could sometimes get a tip of another farthing, particularly if the customer was a long way off. Most people in the district could only afford one delivery of coal per week and the local merchant of Upper Emily Street had about 20 carts. Of a Saturday morning all the boys stood in a long queue and as soon as a cart was filled the first at the head set off with his load. The next had to wait until carts were returned and we all moved up the line. As soon as you had delivered your load you stood again at the end of the queue. On wet cold days sometimes the queue wait was only about a quarter of an hour. All the money we earned went into the family budget.

I attended Upper Highgate School in my early years at Dymoke Street. I used to go to my Grandma Butler's house in Upper Emily Street for my regular midday meals. As her eldest grandson she thought a lot of me. I remember spending a holiday with her at Tardibegge, near Bromsgrove.

My father, working at the Austin factory, used to catch the train at Camp Hill and meet the same people every day.

shillings. I remember Mother used to wheel Vic to the butcher's with me at her side and beg for bones with even a trace of meat. Our meals were stew from the bones with dumplings and potatoes. The only change from this was sausage and mash, followed by bread pudding. On sausage and mash days I am sure Mother used to just eat mashed potatoes. We had to clean our plates so clean with a piece of bread that we could turn them upside down and have the bread pudding on the reverse side. No clean plate, no pudding.

My mother's mother, Gran Dixon, lived at 70 Anderton Road, Small Heath and we used to walk Vic in the pushchair to Gran's. Three of her brothers were at the Post Office and bringing in regular money so we used to obtain meals there. While I was at school my mother used to wheel Vic to Gran's and then walk to her uncle's barber shop, where for very few coppers she used to scrub and clean his windows and living quarters. It was in this fashion that we lasted through the General Strike, with no regular wages coming in.

Another memory of Dymoke Street was the washday ritual. We kept a large barrel in the yard which collected all the rainwater from the roof downspouts. This was used to wash the clothes, as the water was so hard that soap did not produce a lather. Washday meant operating a dolly, a heavy wooden contraption with a large head having slots in the end, a stave and cross-handle at the top. The clothes had to be mashed, punched and slammed with this tool until all the dirt had been removed, then fed through a hand-operated mangle time and time again. Then the washing was hung on clothes lines until dry, and then ironed. I was fully instructed in all these operations and allowed to iron flat pieces of washing, under surveillance. One Saturday, my friend Jim was helping his mother in a similar way and caught his fingers in the mangle. The pressure burst open each finger and blood was everywhere. In under the count of three suddenly the whole street was there, all offering advice and help. This was typical of the district – the slightest breach of peace and everyone flocked to the scene. Someone fetched a pram and he was wheeled to the doctor's, and from there to hospital. His wounds took a very long time to heal.

At Dymoke Street, bath nights of a Friday were a ritual. Vic used to be bathed first in a large metal bath in front of the fire. Water had to be heated by a coal fire in the washhouse and my mother carried one large saucepan at a time, ladled out of the wash boiler. For my turn I had to use the same water, with the addition of an extra saucepan of hot water. My parents also used the same bath, but after we had been sent to bed. It was economical to have one boil-up of the washhouse boiler for the whole family.

The house at Dymoke Street was connected to the gas supply and we had a gas light in our bedroom. We were only allowed to have it on very low, or else a candle, and as I used to read a great deal, I think this dim lighting caused me to have defective eyesight.

By the time of our last Christmas at Dymoke Street the General Strike was over and we suddenly seemed to be better off. Vic and I were bought scooters for Christmas, the best and most expensive presents we had ever had. When the strike finished and all was back to normal, Dad decided to move to King's Heath.

2

School

We moved to 33 Brentford Road, King's Heath about the middle of 1927. My parents were overjoyed to have their own house at last. It had a separate bathroom and toilet and a garden 67 yards long. I have reason to remember the length, for my perpetual job to earn my sixpence pocket money was to dig this from top to bottom every year and keep the one path straight with a row of stones either side.

I remember the very first Sunday we moved in Dad took us on a walk down May Lane to a small grass island at the bottom of the lane and said, 'At last we are in the heart of the country.' As far as the eye could see there were no other buildings or houses of any sort.

Both Vic and I attended Colmore Street School, just over a mile away across fields, paths and country lanes. We had hardly settled in before I sat an entrance exam to King's Norton Secondary School and gained a scholarship there.

The journey to King's Norton Secondary School was quite a trek, involving a walk at either end and a tram and bus ride. After a few months of these trips I was bought a bicycle to ride to and from school. I met up with Jack Cotterill, who also used to cycle, so we became friends.

Soon after starting at King's Norton School I experienced difficulty in reading from the blackboard and had to have an eye test. I was very loath to wear glasses, but finally had to wear them all the time.

I had many clashes with the masters. On one occasion as I walked down the classroom, a grandfather clock which had always stood in the corner suddenly fell and crashed into the bench, just after I had passed, and smashed into smithereens. I swear I passed several feet away and did not touch it at all. Anyway I was lambasted by the master, and had two hours' detention.

I seemed to collect detentions. Once a row of railings fell down when I was talking to my friends. They were leaning against the railing and I was at least a yard from them but the master accused me again and gave me a detention.

Another time I was given a detention for stealing apples from an orchard near the school boundary. The boys used to climb the fence and help themselves. A notice was displayed that severe penalties would be imposed on anyone found climbing the fence. I got a piece of wood and put a large nail in the end, and threading it through the railings was able to collect windfalls. Having supplied all my friends I was caught again, though I had not climbed the fence nor eaten any myself. If ever the ball used at playtime finished on the roof, it always seemed to be me who went to recover it, got caught and was sentenced to detention. In Chemistry when boys mixed up chemicals to cause a small explosion, I was blamed for it; again a detention.

Nevertheless I enjoyed my years at King's Norton, and especially sport, being picked for matches all through the year. I have supported Birmingham City Fooball Club since Dad used to take me to St Andrews. In those days if you didn't arrive early you could not get in the ground. I remember one Boxing Day going to St Andrews a good half-hour before the kick-off against West Bromwich Albion, and we could not even climb the stairs leading to the terraces. Even after the match had started we had only just reached the top of the stairs and were not able to see any of the play. We only saw the ball when it was kicked high in the air. After constant pushing by everybody together it was half-time before Dad could see part of the game when play reached the north end of the field. We learned of the result when supporters started to leave the ground near the close of play. There were times when the south end was enveloped in thick smoke from the trains which passed very close to the ground. It was rumoured that if at any time the Blues were losing, any railway workers unable to attend the match would arrange for a train to remain close to the south stand and direct jets of water onto the hot coals, so that clouds of smoke would obliterate the south end of the ground from view.

One day, at the morning break, we saw the sky alight, and learned later that the R101 had exploded at its mooring in Rugby.

Jack Cotterill and I got up to several pranks; some of them not so funny. We had been to King's Heath Park for a match and meandered over to the railway line on which was a complete train-load of goods trucks ready to be delivered. Seeing a chance to make mischief we climbed over the fence and changed the labels so that the chap ordering pig food would receive a load of timber and the chap expecting timber would receive pig food, and so on. We laughed our heads off at the various combinations until we heard the railway officer approaching and ran off. We only did this as a prank but later realized the problems that could be caused by our foolishness.

At Brentford Road I began piano lessons. Dad thought it would be a good idea to have me learn to play the piano and act as a deputy in Uncle Sid's marathon playing sessions at Anderton Road. My piano lessons were a trial because I was tone deaf and could never play by ear, but only from sheet music. My teacher was Sid Glass, the pianist at the Hippodrome, who played in concerts at the Town Hall. He was very strict and severe. I had to practise one hour every day and in the summer evenings all my pals would wait outside an open window waiting for me to complete my practice. I was for ever altering the one large clock in the house, moving the hands forward just after starting and then back before finishing, so as to get through the hour in about twenty minutes.

I once got in real trouble for missing my piano practice. Having promised to do it on my return, I was allowed out for a cycle ride. We all went off to Mill Pond to explore the derelict mill. On the way home my pedal seized up and screwed itself off as it turned. After screwing it on I could only progress a few yards before the pedal was off again. Instead of arriving home at eight o'clock it was nearly ten when I got back. My father was absolutely furious that I had gone out without having practised the piano. For the first and only time I had to bend over the chair and with bare buttocks had six strokes from my father's trouser belt. I never missed practice again. However, it was a complete waste of time and money, for any interest or natural ability was missing. I was tone deaf, but I would accompany my dad on his favourite songs: One Alone, In a Persian Market and Friend of Mine, strictly from music sheets.

Not long after we had moved to Brentford Road in 1928 my grandmother Butler died of bronchitis. We attended the funeral at Brandwood End Cemetery. I was very fond of my gran and I grieved very much over her death.

For nine years in succession, during our last years at Dymoke Street, and after we moved to Brentford Road, we used to go every August to Rhos-on-Sea and stay at Rose Cottage. (The cottage is still there today, but I never thought all those years ago that I would live in the district.) We all slept in two double beds in the same room, Vic and I in one and Mum and Dad in the other. Once Vic and I caught dozens of small crabs and kept them in sand buckets, which we left outside the back door. The owners of the cottage slept downstairs, and as this night happened to be very warm they had left the back door open. The crabs escaped and swarmed all over the beds and caused mayhem to our hosts.

One year our journey to Rhos was a disaster start to finish. The trouble began on Friday night. Dad had secreted all his savings for the holiday, and suddenly they were missing. Everywhere was searched, the dustbins were all emptied and sifted, no trace anywhere. We all stood still for a silent prayer that we might find them. Then mother said she had a premonition to look in the miskin, and we found them there. We set off at 4.00 a.m. next morning and reached Chester about midday, after many stops, and trouble with the motorcycle engine. In Chester we had a contretemps with a tram which swerved across our path to pick up passengers. We hit the tram; it broke a part of the steering column and we had to stay the night at the local garage man's home while he and his son worked all night to repair the motorcycle for us to travel on to Rhos the next day. We all had to share a double bed, Mother and Dad the top and Vic and me at the bottom with all our feet and arms intertwined.

We set off early next morning and on crossing the bridge into North Wales, a lorry just ahead of us carrying crates of live fowl crashed into another lorry carrying milk churns. What a mess and what a cacophony. Mother made Dad drive on. She said she could not bear to be involved.

On another of these journeys it rained heavily all the way, and the water splashing on to the motorcycle magneto caused it to periodically fail. After cleaning and replacing we made a few more miles, eventually reaching a place called Oakengates. We stopped for an evening meal having travelled all day, and on returning to the combination found the sidecar filled with water. So Dad had no alternative but to leave the cycle, and we all returned home by train.

Dad said never again; sold the combination and bought an

Austin Seven with an umbrella-type canvas roof. At almost the same time George Jennings sold his combination and also bought an Austin Seven. The families then renewed their association and we again made local trips on Sundays, visiting Evesham, Stratford, Malvern, Clent, the Cotswolds, Symonds Yat, Cannock Chase, Lichfield, Nuneaton and many more.

Mother and Dad sometimes used to go to the cinema, leaving Vic and me to do our homework and piano practice. By now Vic was having piano lessons too, and was proving far better than me. I had read in one of my comics the recipe to make ginger beer. I had collected bottles for several weeks and now used one of these nights to produce my own ginger beer. Having made it, bottled it and cleaned up, I placed the bottles in the spare room and retired. In the middle of the night, some of the bottles burst and blew their corks. I woke up to hear Mother shouting hysterically, 'God, what's that, Alf?' Dad was in a hell of a rage and ordered me never again to do such a thing without his permission. Anyway it was nice to have my own ginger beer for a short time from the four bottles that remained.

At about this time my friend Roger Palmer formed a strong friendship with one of the girls from Trettiford Road School. Eileen Cole was a very pretty, vivacious girl and a bit of a tomboy. Her father was manager of a cinema in Bull Ring. Roger and I seemed to spend an increasing amount of time with Eileen and I realized I was getting very fond of her company. Roger and I used to climb a large tree near to her home and watch her house for hours on end just hoping for a glimpse. We managed to become very friendly with her younger brother Len, whom we used to bribe to tell us of her movements.

Roger was a very keen musician and had high hopes of getting into the Marines as a band player. During our time together we tried to think of something we could invent to make our futures. One of our ideas was a vehicle driven by an electric motor, but instead of the spindle being the rotating part, the outer case would revolve. We then watched golfers on Cocksmoor Golf Club carrying clubs and thought we could adapt our idea to build a vehicle that could be geared to carry weight and climb steep hills at a slow pace. We continued to see and speak to Eileen Cole whenever we could. We learnt that on leaving school at Trettiford Road she had obtained a job at Cadbury's and a cycle to get back and forward to work. She had had no help from her parents in finding the money to buy the cycle; her eldest brother who was a petty officer in the Royal Navy had lent it to her. She saved all her pocket money to pay him back. Meanwhile Roger and I both persuaded our parents to get us second-hand cycles. Mine was one of Uncle Sid's which was going cheap.

The time was now approaching for sitting my matriculation exams at King's Norton. Spare time was spent swotting as much as possible and my days and hours seemed fully occupied. On the day of the exams we all sat in the large hall at individual chairs and tables – a process that was to be repeated many, many times during my career. I remember my feelings at each exam, when the questions seemed to be completely different to the ones studied and perfected. For each exam it was the same and I felt my hopes shattered every time.

3

An Austin Apprentice; Girlfriends

My results came through and I had passed my matriculation. I finished school at King's Norton in July 1932 and my father organized my entry as a trade apprentice at Austin Motor Company Ltd. He could not afford at that time to enter me on the full apprenticeship programme, so I enrolled at King's Heath night school, where because my matric. results exempted me from the first year I went straight into the second year. At the end of my first year at night school the results were such that the head sent for Dad and said they could not fully develop my potential. I sat a further exam and gained entrance to the full apprenticeship scheme, leading to becoming a toolmaker at Austin Motor Company, and I enrolled on the mechanical production degree course at Suffolk Street College. A similar scheme was awarded to a close friend, Douglas Hague, and we both entered our careers at the same time. Our studies and pursuits were destined to run parallel.

In those days, day release was not available so classes had to be four nights a week with the weekend to be used for homework and writing up laboratory experiments.

During my attendance at King's Heath, on our way to night school, Roger and I both used a detour near Eileen's place, in the hope of seeing her. On one of these occasions Roger's bike had a puncture and I was scooting alongside him on the pavement. Suddenly a Post Office van travelling at speed hit me, carried me forward on the bonnet and tossed me into the road, hitting the middle of my forehead on the corner of the kerb. I did a forward roll and finished with a split head, pouring blood. The driver returned and took me to the nearest doctor, who immediately sent me to the accident hospital in Bath Row. Apparently the van driver had not finished his training and on this occasion was running very late on his scheduled round.

I had sixteen stitches in my head and was in hospital for two weeks. Father claimed compensation but because it was a government concern was persuaded to accept an out-of-court offer, sufficient to pay for a new racing cycle, hand-built by a racing specialist. It was a super-light cycle with derailleur gears and built to a racing trim.

In the summer, having fully recovered, Eileen and I used to go on many cycle rides together. One Sunday we set off early and rode to see Eileen's Auntie Mabel and Uncle Jack at Malvern, returning after tea. We also used to ride to Evesham, Stratford and the Cotswolds.

For some time Mother and Dad had been trying to talk me into making a date with Eileen Jennings. Both families had hoped from the early days that since one family had two sons and the other two daughters of approximately the same age, that there might be the possibility of arranging a closer union. One day it was arranged for Eileen to travel from Aston to King's Heath; I was to meet her, take her for tea and a chat and take her back to her bus. Dad gave me £5 to spend, which in those days was quite a lot of money. I bought a box of chocolates, met her, went for a stroll and took her for tea and cakes. All the time she was trying to find if there was a possible future for us. I told her of my friend Roger and his girlfriend, also Eileen, that I thought a great deal of her and as Roger was expecting to join the Marines shortly I hoped to make her my own girlfriend. I think this was an important crossroads in my life. I felt my fortune lay with Eileen Cole, and told Eileen Jennings so. She was very upset, and I could do nothing to soothe her feelings. So we parted that day with a sort of finality. I felt sorry later that I had let her down so badly.

On my return Mother and Dad wanted a full report, and said the best thing I could do was invite Eileen Cole to meet them. I had to stall because I felt I had crossed a bridge too far, too soon.

Roger Palmer had received details of his enrolment and was now equipped with his uniform: dark blue, with silver buttons and cap. He looked splendid, was the envy of the lads and the darling of all the girls. He had about two weeks of glory before joining his unit. Soon after he left, Ken Middleton took over as escort to Eileen Cole. At that time several of Eileen's friends made a fuss of me, but on my side it was only mild friendship, my heart was somewhere else. One evening, riding my bike through the Dingles I saw Eileen on the opposite bank, walking with Ken. She suddenly pointed to me on the other side and said to Ken, 'There is the man I am going to marry.' From then on my destiny was fixed. We spent as much time as possible together. I was introduced to her family and her mother took an instant liking to me. By now I was involved in more studies, and had to attend night school at Suffolk Street four nights a week. Eileen used to travel to town on the bus to wait for me, just for the company on the bus back to her home. I now arranged for Eileen to meet my family; the meeting was an instant success. On this first occasion Dad suggested we all played cards, solo and bridge. Eileeen reported to her family, 'The Shelleys are all right, but they're mad on cards.' Time was to confirm this impression.

In my first days at the Austin Motor Company I met all my fellow workers on the machine tool recondition department. I was assigned as apprentice to Horace Trueman, a key skilled man in the department, but he happened to be away ill for my first month, so I was directed to all sorts of jobs; sweeping the floors, fetching and carrying. My first real task was to clean down a machine withdrawn from production after about 12 years hard work. The filth, grime and grease was unbelievable. After the top surface had been cleaned the fitters completely stripped every removable part down to the name-plate. The whole lot was then immersed in a degreasing tank, but the body of the machine had to be cleaned and scraped by hand. My overalls were so filthy that mother swore they would stand up on their own.

The next job to learn was scrapping. Master level plates were blued and pushed back and forward over the top slides and all the high spots removed until a universal mottled appearance signalled the slides were perfectly flat. If this perfect surface were left overnight, by the next morning distortion had taken place and the whole process had to be repeated. The next operation was to scrape the mating part to equal standards. After each stage an inspector had to be called to pass the recondition, and all parts of the machine were checked for wear or play. Orders were then sent to the machine shop to complete repairs on all working parts. Only when the machine and its slides were square, flat and true did the interesting part of reassembly take place. There was a great deal of job satisfaction in watching a machine discarded as scrap repaired and performing to 100 per cent efficiency.

I came in for a lot of leg-pulling and pranks – like the day I was sent to the stores for the long weight and spent a long time waiting to be served. I was once sent for the glass hammer; and I returned with a hammer with a plastic head and so reversed the leg-pull. Once I was given a suds tank to clean out. The chap that asked me said he'd dropped sixpence in it, which I could keep if I found it when the tank was clean – once he'd found half a crown. By such ruses they were able to get some of their dirtiest jobs done.

After my first year in the machine shop, I was moved to the west press shop, on try-out and development, while my father was promoted to tool room superintendent. He had studied under a double-action press tool specialist from the USA and had a natural ability to feel with his hands the metal strains in a pressing. He became an expert on double-action press tools and pressings, and was sought after by many firms in the country: Fords at Dagenham, Pressed Steel at Oxford, Bliss Presses, Toledo Presses and Fisher and Ludlow. His advice was always respected. He used to take me back to the press shops on a Sunday afternoon and spend hours and hours trying to teach me his skill, but to no avail. I could not feel a thing, try as I might. He cursed and ranted at me but I could not absorb his skill.

My job in press tool development consisting of coaxing a successful panel from the double-action presses. One of my first jobs was making the Austin Seven back panel. This had previously been produced in several pieces and welded together. Now, for the first time, the panel was to be produced complete, in one blow of the press. Because of the size of the tool, I had to roll into it below floor level, when its top and bottom halves were jacked apart, and either increased the radius of the window light or change the shape of the punch. There was very little room to move and all the metal removed fell on my face. I began to feel some sympathy for Victorian chimney sweeps' boys.

After I had rolled out of the tool another panel was struck, and again my dad applied his skill and determined the next stage of adjustment. We would either alter the pressure settings in certain positions of the outer rings, or increase the radii, and in certain places create beads and corresponding bead channels to help control the metal flow. I was intrigued by the determination of these channels. Once their position and size were decided, centre pops were made with a centre punch along the exact line of the bead. A small ball bearing was placed in the centre pop. The two pressure rings were then closed and a perfect reproduction made on both rings for the placing of the bead and bead channel. The tool was unfastened from the press, taken out and the upper ring inverted. Then the attachment of the bead in the upper ring was carried out, and the channel in the bottom tool was similarly created with chisels, grinding and filing to an exact depth and form gauge. It was absolutely staggering to me that when the tools were refitted, with the adjustments made, that perfect panels were the result.

Being the youngest in the department, I was appointed tea boy, responsible for taking the tin billycans already filled with tea, sugar and condensed milk to the hot water supply. In the queue were several dozen boys like myself on similar errands, all moaning about the ignominy of making tea. I considered this, and made plans to capitalize on the arrangement. I set up a stock of various teas, sugars and condensed milk and offered a complete service three times a day. I made myself a wooden yoke like a milkmaid's which could carry some twenty cans at a time. I then solicited for custom from the production departments, and obtained a full order book. I only had the tea-breaks in which to complete my round; sometimes I had to work right through my dinner-break organizing things. I kept accounts and cleared my turnover of the money every Friday. By now the other boys retired from competition and I had more orders than I could manage. In two years I made over £30 and bought my first car, a little Austin Seven, six years old, for £29. I now gave up my tea round and spent all my spare time stripping, cleaning, replacing parts and caring for my pride and joy.

During the winter when I had to attend four nights a week at Suffolk College, I had been catching the tram at Longbridge at 6.30 p.m. to be at school for 7.00 p.m. and every night without fail slept on the tram and was woken at Suffolk Street terminus just outside the college by the conductor who said 'Right, school time for you.' With my own car it became easier to go to and from night school, and Eileen used to meet me for the drive back home. We also used to go out for rides, and after a time I taught her to drive.

Whilst serving my first year in the machine repair section, I became friendly with a fitter, Jack Goodwin. Jack was a fitness fanatic and always talking of running and cross-country jogs. After some time he finally persuaded me to join him in a Saturday afternoon work-out. Straight after work on this Saturday, we changed in a room used by the Austin Harriers underneath the snooker room reserved for the senior staff. It was equipped with showers, tables, changing benches and rows of coat-hangers. I only had pumps and football kit; Jack proudly wore his Birchfield Harrier jersey. He had decided to do four laps of the testing track round the perimeter of the airfield, and I surprised myself by keeping pace with him – only when he ran his finishing sprint did he leave me behind. The outcome of this new experience was that I also became addicted to the sport. Soon I was a member of Austin Harriers and Birchfield Harriers; regular Saturday afternoons were then spent on cross-country running or training sessions. Austin Harriers were a member of Cross-Country Business Houses League and ran against other large factory teams; we ran home and away contests all over the Midlands. There was also a triangular contest with Harbourne and Evesham. At one of these meetings, held in deep winter at Evesham, the course was across newly ploughed fields heavy with mud and was a strict test of stamina. I was third, behind Joe Holden of Tipton and John Shaw of Harbourne, when we crossed a field with bulls at rest. Suddenly seeing streams of colour-vested runners disturbing their peace roused these fierce-looking beasts, and one decided his target would be John Shaw. He made a beeline for him. John changed course towards the River Avon, but the brute followed him. Without more ado John leapt into the river and stood armpit-deep, shouting, while the bull ventured as near as he could. The rest of us collapsed in laughter; John never lived down that day.

After I joined Birchfield Harriers I was enrolled for road running sessions on my free night, Wednesday, which happened to be their training night. Jack Richards took an interest in me and helped to coach me. I was selected one year to run one of the legs of the London to Brighton run, and also one of the legs of the Preston to Blackpool road relay races. I performed creditably and held my place each time. My schooling came first and I had to turn down many other opportunities. I was appointed first reserve to the Everill Cup team and attended the competition at Arley. Jack Goodwin finished sixth of the team of twelve which won the event, and treasured his gold medal.

There was one occasion that affected my progress as a running athlete. I was picked in the team to compete against Birmingham University team to be held over a cross-country course starting at headquarters at Perry Bar. On this Saturday after finishing work and getting home, I had to wait for Vic who had borrowed my cycle. When he arrived I had only about three-quarters of an hour to cycle from King's Heath, through city centre, to Perry Bar. He had been riding my bike up and down the pavements and his pals had been shooting arrows from bows in and out of the spokes of the wheels. Consequently the wheels were bent and intermittently caught on the brakes. The ride over was tortuous up hills, and I had to pedal even downhill. I arrived at the ground to find all the runners assembled at the start line. The trainer and manager helped me to get ready, and held back the start. I set off still unsettled from my ride, but managed to stay in third place behind two University lads over the seven-mile course. Cantering through the last hedge, close behind the two in front, the branches they pushed out of their way sprang back and hit me on the head. I reached the road about five yards behind the second and twenty yards behind the leader. I remember jogging down the road with both the front runners oscillating in my dim conscious state. I know I passed the second athlete and was making a last effort for the lead, but I do not remember any more. Apparently I drew level near the finish, but the Birchfield trainer saw that I was heading for a brick wall and ran forward and caught me. I came to with the trainer massaging me, and the club completely empty except for us. When I had recovered I set off for home on my cycle. I finally arrived home and a complete physical check-up was arranged for Monday afternoon. No damage had occurred but the doctor suggested I take up an alternative sport for a couple of years.

I joined the Cocksmoor Woods Football Club and as a member of the Birmingham Intermediate League we played clubs all over the Midlands: I was persuaded to play goal and although handicapped by playing without glasses, performed reasonably well. So much so, I was selected to play for the Provisionals against the Probables in order to select a team to represent the League in a knockout competition for Birmingham Lord Mayor's Cup. I remember one of the matches against a strong team from Kalamazoo. Their forwards were five strapping chaps built more for rugby than soccer. We were overwhelmed and lost 5-0. Everyone praised me for my performance, but I finished limping; I had torn a thigh muscle, so was out for over two weeks. We also played friendly matches against Monyhull Colony and Hampton-in-Arden. Both were institutions for the mentally handicapped. The only games the warden and staff could play were against teams that were prepared to visit them. The match we played against Hampton was memorable. For the first time we played in front of a full house of spectators. They were eight deep all round the touchline and in goal I was surrounded by a hundred or so gibbering patients whom I had a job to keep out of goal. Whenever their team attacked the noise was terrific. After the match we were shown some dangerous inmates kept in cages; wardens, we were told, had to enter in pairs because of the ferocity of their attacks.

When Dad changed his car to a brand new Austin, he decided that we needed a separate garage, and started to look for another house. One of the fitters in the press tool room had his house for sale at 83 Midhurst Road, King's Norton, and when Dad heard of this, he visited the house, and decided to buy – the garage had room for two cars. The back garden was as large as at Brentford Road and once more I had the job of digging it over. It had only been about a third cultivated. Dad bought himself a greenhouse which became his pride and joy. He asked advice from everybody under the sun and tried to carry out all suggestions made to him: paraffin heaters, mulch pots, power cables, lighting. Meanwhile, in doing the digging, we had discovered that the site was across an old ditch, so that water was continually draining from under the house. Dad built a draining pool in the garden and arranged a permanently working pump, but the pool still filled. Finally he was persuaded to sink sleepers in the ground at the point where the ditch entered the garden, and seal these with tar. This proved effective, but the next door garden then had its share of water doubled. They didn't bother cultivating their garden; it remained a marshland and the water continued to run down the road.

My progress continued and finally I obtained my Higher National Certificate. When the results were discussed the head of engineering told me that my strength of materials paper was well worth a distinction – unfortunately the examiner disagreed; that would have meant me finishing top of all 900 Austin apprentices. I came second, and my close friend Doug Hague third. However the results of my practical tests and remarks of my tutor enabled me to be elected Apprentice of the Year of the Austin Motor Company. Lord Austin sent for me and presented me with a gold hunter watch, suitably inscribed. Doug Hague was also given a gold watch. I learned that my success was further to be rewarded at a ceremony organised by the Production Engineers, where I was to be introduced to the Duke and Duchess of York.

To celebrate my 21st birthday I organized a coach tour from Cotteridge to Sutton, picking up the Jennings family and Eileen Cole and her mother en route. We finished at a small hotel at Four Oaks, where I had reserved a room with a buffet meal provided. I received many useful presents which I still use to this day. Eileen bought me an engraved ring. I only wore it for a short time, as one day drilling metal at work a piece of swarf got trapped in the ring and I nearly lost my finger. I felt unsure about wearing it again, but keep it as a memento.

Vic progressed tremendously well at King's Norton and was appointed captain of both soccer and cricket teams. He had developed into a six-foot, bronzed, healthy athlete. In the Whitsun of his last year at school we all went on holiday to Bournemouth with Mr and Mrs Jennings, Sybil and Eileen Cole, by now my steady girlfriend. On this holiday a strong bond grew between Vic and Sybil; seeing them together there could be no doubt a deep affection had developed. Mother, Dad and the Jenningses were delighted.

On our return Vic had to sit his final matriculation exams. Dad had made provisional plans for him to serve an apprenticeship in electronics in the research department attached to Dad's toolroom and under his control. The week following his exams Dad arranged for Vic to start work in the stores, so that he would be familiar with the electricians' terms and requirements. His apprenticeship was to start on his 16th birthday. That week, Vic and I both worked at laying a lawn in the back garden at Midhurst Road, taking turns at ramming the turfs flat with boards. Vic asked me if he could borrow my car on the Saturday to attend a friend's wedding, and I agreed. At work on Saturday morning I called over at mid-morning lunch-break to see how he was getting on and he asked me to eat his sweet for him, knowing how upset Mum would be if it were left.

Returning home on Saturday evening I was surprised to see my car still outside. Mum and Dad had gone out. Vic was slouched on the settee; he said he felt a bit queasy and had not gone to the wedding. He went off to bed and made me swear not to tell Mum and Dad. He had never had a day's illness in his life and I was deeply concerned. I waited up for our parents and said Vic seemed a bit off colour and had gone to bed.

First thing on Sunday morning, Dad questioned him and said, 'That's the first time in your life you have complained of being unwell. Off to the doctor's.'

Dr Paynes saw him at his private house and immediately got Vic into hospital. He was operated on that night for appendicitis. The surgeon said he had very little chance as the appendix had burst. I had the same blood group as Vic and gave a transfusion on Monday night, lying next to his still, pale figure. I asked them to take all they needed to save him. Vic died late Tuesday afternoon.

This was a tragic blow to the family; it was so unbelievably sudden. We had to keep Mother and Dad separate from one another, and tried to keep them occupied. After the funeral on Friday the Austin Company loaned Dad one of their limousines, and gave him indefinite leave. Gran Dixon and Aunty Vin were with us, and straight after the funeral I drove this car, with all of us in it, for a week in Brighton. This week was the most difficult time I had ever spent. The tragedy filled our lives.

It also greatly affected Sybil Jennings. She was heart-broken and vowed never to marry; Vic was her one and only love. In fact, she never did give up mourning. She married eventually very late in life, but in all those years the memory of a brief but intense affection seemed all she wanted.

Some time later one of the neighbours came to Mother and said that her son, a great pal of Vic's, had told them a few weeks before the tragedy, his group of friends, including Vic, had a competition to see who could swallow the most plum stones. Vic had won, swallowing 16 stones and collecting a halfpenny from each of his friends. Had he put his life in danger for eightpence? Some doctors said this could not have been responsible; but the thought in all our minds was that plum stones quickly swallowed in succession could have triggered his appendicitis. I, of course, dwelt on the stamping of that lawn a week earlier, and how he might have been in pain, but shrugged it off.

We returned to the grave on Vic's birthday. A distant hooter sounded for the end of the day shift at Austin's. Dad said, 'This would have been his first week as an electrician apprentice.' It is one of my most poignant memories.

On our return, Dad was confined to bed. I had the task of trying to run his job, taking messages and instructions to his widespread heads of department, returning with numerous requests and appeals for decisions. This went on for over a month. I was facing my fifth year of apprenticeship and the lead-up to my Higher National Degree, plus the various endorsements required to complete my training. I suppose this affected my health, for I had an attack of yellow jaundice and had to go away for a week to Tyn-y-Groes Hospital in Llandudno. I called to see our old friends who were still at Rose Cottage at Rhos-on-Sea during my stay.

Dad resumed work, but was only a shadow of his former self. By now I had progressed from a tool-maker in the press tool room to my final year as a tool designer in the drawing office, first designing press tools and then in jigs and fixture design. I was still regularly attending four nights a week at night school.

4

Sports and Courtship

After five years at Austin's, Dad suggested I applied to the firm to purchase a new car through the employees' discount scheme. I found that I could buy a brand new Austin Seven saloon right off the production line, taxed and insured for the year, for £98.

I sold my old car for £42, added my savings and borrowed the rest from Mother. I paid her back at £2 a week; as my apprenticeship was now complete I earned the princely sum of £5 a week.

To celebrate the new car I took Eileen and her mother for the first spin; we went to Ashby-de-la-Zouche for a drink. Eileen's mother obtained a rug for the car, and made two cushions for me to match the green upholstery of the car.

I came very much closer in friendship to Doug Hague. We worked in the same office, had finished our exams together and were both keen on sports. Doug was a very keen racing cyclist. Once, after work on Saturday morning, he bought a new gear sprocket, fixed it to his bike and cycled off to try it out. He cycled to Aberystwyth and back in the afternoon and evening – more than 200 miles.

We were now entering open meetings, Doug and his brother Charles cycling for Weoley Castle Wheelers and Don Marlowe and I running. I was also a member of Small Heath Harriers. We attended races all over the Midlands, each of us winning various prizes, and getting together to decide which event we would invest stake money in order to return our full expenses. The bookies were always keen to collect money from athletes; they offered generous odds because they then knew who was really trying to win.

Our best day was at Bristol Kingswood open meeting. We all worked at Austin Motor Company and after finishing work at midday on Saturday, set off in my Austin Seven with a full load of four athletes, all their kit and two cycles strapped to the back of the car. All the boys changed into their racing kit en route and I with their help managed mine, with only my accelerator-pedal foot without its spiked shoe. We arrived at Kingswood just in time. The runners for my heat were being assembled, and I was the first to compete in the 440 yards. We had a wonderfully successful day. I won the 440 yards final, Don Marlow was second; we finished second and third in the half mile; Don won the mile and I was third. The two Hagues cleared the two cycling events as well as coming first and second in the invitation five-mile event, and winning all the lap prizes. We had backed ourselves in various events, and finished with a car full of prizes and £12 each in our pockets. We bought a case of bottled beer and just outside Alcester at way after midnight we finished the beer.

The next Saturday we were entered in Long Eaton open. We set off as before and on reaching Castle Donnington we pulled up behind a festival procession. Suddenly a car crashed into our rear and rendered the bikes unridable. I also hit my knee on the glove box and was unable to run. Doug and Charles managed to borrow a bike, but this was our low day. We came back with only one prize, no winnings, a damaged car and two damaged cycles.

Dad now expressed a wish to see me run and brought Eileen along with him to the Cheltenham open. Everyone wanted to know which event I meant to really go for; I told them the half mile. The event was staged in three heats, the first three runners in each heat entering the final. Near the home straight in my heat I saw about six runners in front of me, so I sprinted and won. Dad hadn't bet on the heat, but now after my winning it he could not get any bookies to take a bet on the final. I felt good in the race and at the home bend could hear my dad, over all the hundreds in the crowd, shout, 'It's in the bag.' I just slightly relaxed. The next thing I knew I was being passed by John Beck, and finished second. He told us that he had just returned from army training in Egypt and had done all his training running on the loose sand of the desert. It must have improved his strength for I could not match his finish.

I had now given up all football, and in the winter continued with cross-country running. I was in training for the Everill Cup Race to be held over seven miles cross country at Stratford. I won the trial race at Birchfield and was among the first twelve selected to represent the club. Medals were available to the six best runners in the first three teams. Both Dad and Eileen came to watch me for their first cross-country meeting. It was a very wet, heavy course and for some reason I just could not get going. Although Birchfield won the team event I was only seventh in the team, so did not get a medal. The next Saturday I won the Birchfield Harriers open meeting and had a medal for that. So much for the ups and downs of athletics.

One evening in December 1937, Eileen and I went to the cinema, and returning on the bus, alone together on the top deck, I knelt in the gangway and proposed marriage to her. She accepted. I knew her mother would be pleased at our engagement. The first chance I had I spoke to her father and asked for his approval, which he gave, though surprised that I had asked him. He thought all those customs were not now observed.

I now attended night school only one night a week for endorsements to my degree. I also did training one night a week, and Don Marlow, Doug and Charles Hague and myself used to spend one night a week meeting at Weoley Castle and walking together along the country lanes to Bell Broughton or Frankley. We used to sing all the songs we knew, and some we didn't, at the top of our voices, have just one round of drinks, and repeat the voice training all the way back, jumping and leaping to try and touch the leaves of the trees as we passed by.

A trip was arranged to visit Aberfan in South Wales with Eileen and her mother to see their relations. It was an enjoyable experience to meet Cliff, Granny and Grandad White. Granny White was sweet; she would try to read something in the paper and say, 'I can't do it, these glasses have got too young for me.' She wasn't too old, no fear.

Cliff was a miner and was always playing cards for money. He told us the miners on a Friday often gambled their full week's wages away, not an hour after being paid, and remained broke for the week. Their wives learned to save enough from the better days to feed the family and pay the bills.

The cottage at Aberfan was close to the pit, and there was nothing so moving of a winter evening as watching the slow file of miners walking away from the pit, their lanterns swinging in the dusk. Someone ahead would start a song and it would grow and swell back through the ranks until virtually the whole valley would resound in song. It was a never-to-be-forgotten memory.

Eileen's grandparents used to be in service to some great nobleman and I loved to sit and listen to them recount their memories and experiences. Eileen's mother Ada and her sister Mabel were also in service, and together with Cliff and his tales of his experiences underground they used to hold me in raptures. We went many times to South Wales, sometimes with Eileen's mother, or her brother and his girlfriend, or on our own. It was a different world.

Eileen was born next door to Granny White's cottage, and had broken her nose running down the gigantic tip at the back of it. She attended the school at Aberfan, the scene of the tragic disaster that occurred many years later, which involved two of her nephews and a niece.

I had finished all my apprenticeship involvements at Austin Motor Company and was offered several good appointments within the firm, but I felt I wanted to gain extra experience. My father arranged several interviews for me and I could have chosen from a number of posts. At about this time, March 1938, there was news of an aeroplane factory being developed at Dunlop Works, Tyburn. I attended an interview there and was immediately offered a job, to start the following Monday. I found I was only the third employee to be engaged; there was a manager, Mr Day, and one other draughtsman. I was immediately handed the project of planning and designing equipment to produce the Spitfire engine mounting. Every week more and more staff joined the company. We were working in an old wooden store-shed belonging to Dunlop, but this was the start of Castle Bromwich Aeroplane Company, making production-built Spitfires. I soon had eight draughtsmen working for me and was appointed section leader.

We were given the rough sketches and plans of Abe Mitchell. In his early drawings of the plane Abe specified the schedules of the wings; the joining of the projection lines of the dihedrals were to coincide 200 yards each side of the centre fuselage and 400 yards dead ahead for the body trim shape. We were also given details of the engine size and told that our design would have to allow for the possibility of an increase in power in the Merlin engines. In fact 16 progressively stronger and more powerful engines were developed, but no changes were made to our original engine mounting.

There were no computers or calculators in those days so all calculations had to be made in long-hand; using tables we were able to handle nine places of decimals. Our first job was to formulate, design and develop the main pick-up points to carry wing plug and socket engine-fastenings, bulkhead locations and propeller-shaft bearing housings. The section continued to design a checking fixture, to include all the salient locations points. When complete the jig was ordered, at an estimated cost of £20,000. Before the jig was delivered, production ordered twelve to be available, one to remain as a master only. We were all anxious and deeply conscious of the consequences of any mistake. The first fixture was delivered and Southampton sent up a sample engine-mounting that was reported to be perfect. If it fitted in the fixture all would be well. The position of the mounting was established and all gate position and plungers slapped home one at a time. Only one seemed in error. The engine mounting was then set up and a very small fault found in the original pattern. This fault coincided with an error of .009 inches we had found on the dimensions of the drawings supplied by Super Marine. I had sent my calculation to Super Marine and they agreed with my correction. When the sample was corrected, the jig was absolutely perfect, to our great relief.

Ever since Eileen and I had become engaged I had kept a book recording every penny I spent. I tried to save £5 a week, and every Friday night Eileen and I set aside five shillings each to spend on things for our future; pegs, bowl, scrubbing brushes, a broom, a mop, a bucket. One week we selected a pair of steps and had to wait until the following Friday before we could collect them, as they cost £1. We also saved up for items of furniture and marked them off when we had saved enough. The money was kept in the Municipal Bank, earning interest, near where we hoped to live.

I now approached Mr Day for a rise. He said I was already being paid well over the rate at £7.10 shillings per week. I said that if a rise was not forthcoming by the next Friday, I would seek other employment. On Friday he said he had applied for a rise for me but had no news. So I went to B.S.A., was interviewed and obtained an appointment as a planning engineer at a salary of £10 per week. Returning and handing in my notice to Mr Day, he informed me that my rise had come through. It would have been £12 a week.

I started at B.S.A. in April 1939 and worked on the next drawing board to a Ray King. I soon became one of a gang of seven, who used to go out regularly on a Friday night. Once we booked seats in the Empire Theatre, Hurst Street. We had already had a few drinks before getting to the show and in the interval were drinking in the theatre bar. Perhaps our jokes and laughter sounded a little boisterous, for trooping back to our seats we were stopped by the manager and quietly ushered outside – except for Ray King, who had gone to the toilet. He sat through the second half on his own in a row of seats, minding all our coats. Another time we ganged up in Hurst Street and went in and out of all the pubs in single file, swinging our arms and singing 'The Germans are coming, Hooray, Hooray.' A few months later we looked back and regretted our behaviour.

I used to travel to B.S.A. from Midhurst Road in my car, and from work went across to Erdington to see the Coles. I had a lot to do with Eileen's brothers, Len and Cecil. I remember staying there one night and sleeping in a double bed with them both. Before going to bed we had as usual waited up for their father to finish his duties as manager of the Mayfair Cinema. After supper he would try to start an argument, on any subject, which would go on until the early hours.

Eileen's mother died of cancer in May 1938, causing great sorrow in the family. In August of that year Mr Cole and I booked a week's holiday in Blackpool. We spent a lot of the time on the golf course, as Mr Cole had expressed a desire to learn golf. I had only just started to take up the game myself. My first experience of golf was caddying for my dad, and my first shot was on the third hole of the old Redditch course across a valley to the green at the other side. By an absolute fluke it made the green. This was sufficient to sow the seeds of an interest in golf.

Eileen and I began to look for a place to live. We had always been fond of the Dingles, and walking down there one day noticed building being started close by. We learnt that an estate was being developed. The first road, Glen Rise, had a show house; when it was finished we were conducted over it. We liked the area and the house. These houses were being sold for £385 and a deposit of £38 would secure one. We settled on number 46.

We scraped together the deposit and arranged with the Municipal Bank to advance the mortgage. With the help of Aunt Vin and Mother we obtained a bedroom suite, dining suite, lounge suite, fireside armchairs, carpets and curtains for less than £100. We planned to marry after the house was finished in September 1939. Meanwhile we visited the site whenever possible and took photographs as the building developed.

My father had talked to me of the possibility of war. I was still living at Midhurst Road and I remember working on the Sunday that war was declared. I had cycled that day, and as the siren sounded, was just passing Trittiford Park.

5

Marriage and War

Eileen and I were married at King's Norton Church on 21st October, 1939. On the morning of the wedding I went to number 46, lit fires and set the house to rights, then returned to Midhurst Road and cleaned the car. Doug Hague was my best man. The reception was at Cadbury's Social Club at Bournville. We spent our first night in our own home, but after all our expenditure I had fourpence in my pocket to last the week, so we went to Mother's at Midhurst Road for Sunday lunch. We had no time or money for a honeymoon. Soon after we were married Eileen attended a fortune-teller with some friends, just for a joke. She was told that she would have a good life, want for nothing at all, and everything she asked for she would get. She would have three children and she would live to be 75 years old. The fortune-teller also said, 'I am sorry, my love, but I cannot see anything beyond that.' To Eileen, at 21 years old, that seemed a very long way off. She was happy to accept the prediction.

We did have three wonderful children; our daughters Bobbie and Pat, and David, our son. Eileen did have everything she asked for and had a good life.

Early in 1940, after about eight months in the drawing office at B.S.A., I was asked if I was interested in a vacancy for an assistant foreman in the department producing Browning guns. I agreed and joined a team of one foreman and four assistant foremen. Almost before I had time to settle in one assistant foreman was posted elsewhere and another promoted to night foreman. A factory unit then opened at Smethwick and the foreman and third assistant foreman were transferred there, which only left me. So suddenly from being an assistant foreman I was undertaking the duties of a foreman and four assistants as well as being responsible for the night shift. I was then called to a meeting and told that production was to be increased fourfold, and that I had the overriding control of ordering machine tools, jig fixtures, floor space and personnel to cope. No sooner had I worked out the details, than orders came to double requirements again, to eight times the original. A factory in Merthyr Tydfil was to produce a complete duplicate plant, in case of emergency action. So my original department was increased sixteen times. I hardly knew what I was doing during those days. Every morning there were queues of workmen, fitters and setters outside my office. I had the night shift production to assess, and the day's targets to work out. I worked through the day and linked up with the night shift and set programme and performance schedules. At about this time I joined the B.S.A. Auxiliary Fire Service (A.F.S.) and put into practice the fire training I had received at Tyn-y-Groes convalescent home at Llandudno. I was promoted to section leader of a fire detail, which meant one night a week on all-night fire duty – on top of a full day's work.

Mr Wood was appointed production manager of the new section and was very insistent on reducing scrap, as a matter of national interest. One particular operation in our section consisted of 119 separate operations on the breach block, so machine errors were very expensive. Introducing a manual process at operation stage meant that a large saving of scrap could be made. The man who did this was a very old, extremely skilful fitter who unfortunately lived in Wolverhampton and in order to catch his train home every night had to leave a few minutes early. He was given permission by my predecessors to slip away early. One night he was accosted by Mr Wood, who immediately sacked him. When I was told I asked the man to return next day. I spent most of that day trying to trace Mr Wood and left messages everywhere. Next day Mr Wood sent for me, told me I had gone behind his back and had me transferred back to the drawing office. I was only back a week before I was transferred to assist the supervisor of the 'old side', which included the barrel mill and the anti-tank gun division.

The night of the barrel mill bombing I was on duty in the A.F.S. We worked all night on the fire. During the conflagration, while the sperm oil used by the mill exploded and blazed, we heard a plane which had been brought down by anti-aircraft balloon crash into the centre of the fire. It was a German Messerschmitt. The pilot, realizing the plane was doomed, and to avoid a heavily congested residential area, flew straight into the blaze. The ammunition from his guns then exploded as he crashed. Remarkably, a photograph of him with his wife taken in the Black Forest fell out with a sealed letter addressed to his wife. Our leader did not open this, but had it posted. I wish I could have copied the address. I got home about 10.00 a.m. next day. Eileen could not recognize me. I had to strip off in the garage, take a bath and then go to bed. I went back to work in the afternoon. That night whilst the Home Guard were on duty and the fire still blazed on, German aircraft strafed the area with machine guns, hoping to catch personnel still on duty. Several Home Guards were injured from gunshot wounds. There was a hue and cry for it was believed a single light had been signalling from the window of the toilet just outside C Block.

I joined the Home Guard after the barrel mill bombing. After work we all collected in the canteen for a meal before being allocated our shifts and appointed our area of guard duty. We were divided into three four-hour shifts from 8 to

12, 12 to 4 and 4 to 8, and we snatched sleep at the off-duty times.

Most of my colleagues from the drawing office joined the Home Guard. One lunchtime we all decided to call at the local employment agency and seek to enlist in the Navy as artificers. The clerk there knew us all, informed us that we could not enlist and furthermore if we did not return to work on our exempt duties he would prosecute us all.

One night we were on duty for the last two shifts, but free for the first, from 8 to 12. So we all went to the Belgrave Hotel, where we knew they had a snooker table upstairs. The manager said we were welcome to go up, but there were no lights because of blackout restrictions. We prepared to play by the light of torches which we all carried. Just as you were about to pot a ball the torch would be snatched away leaving you in complete darkness, only able to tell if you had potted the ball by the sound. The room had not been dusted for ages. So with dust everywhere, no lights and air raid warnings sounding, we enjoyed ourselves, had a good laugh and returned to duty in time for our shifts. My time was 12 to 4, on the barrel mill surround, the same area that had been attacked the night before. It was a bright moonlight night and we expected a repeat. I was wakened just on midnight by the orderly; it had been reported that the light was still being shown from the toilet, and I was sent to investigate. On my way there the sirens sounded and loudspeakers announced 'All Home Guard take cover'. German bombers were circling overhead in the clear moonlit sky. The barrel mill would have been obvious at the junction of the railway line and the canal.

I had to traverse a path between smouldering heaps of machinery making loud ticking noises as the molten metal cooled, shrank and settled back to the ground. The path I trod was strewn with broken glass and my army boots made a loud noise as I crunched along. As I approached the toilets I felt the real grip of fright. Bombers overhead, an unknown someone ahead, probably armed, who could hear every move I made and to whom I was probably clearly silhouetted. I approached expecting these to be my very last moments on earth. As I lurched open the door of each cubicle I expected the worst. I had a 'bullet up the spout', as the saying goes, and I think I would have shot at any shadow that moved. I found nothing in the toilets and retreated back to my post.

The very next night two Home Guards on patrol did indeed capture a spy, unarmed, but equipped with a powerful torch, from the very same toilet block.

I wonder if on my visit he was there, perhaps hiding in the roof rafters. I shall never know. But the incident remained with me for days. I was truly frightened at the time of my search.

I had maintained close friendship with Ray King, and whenever we had a Saturday afternoon to spare we played at Coxmoor Woods Golf Club, and later at Gay Hill. The course at Gay Hill had two narrow brooks meandering across the course. The field had been commandeered for agricultural use, the fairways had horse drays and carts positioned to prevent enemy aircraft landing. We both resolved to join Gay Hill. The secretary, Les Tyler, told us that the committee had raised the price of subscriptions from £3 to £3.3s.0d, so for the half year our subscription would be £1.12s.6d and the club was pleased to accept us.

My next door neighbour was a member of the A.F.S., appointed to a depot in Brook Lane. Having heard some of my experiences at B.S.A. he enrolled me in his section. One night we were called out to a fire in Bradford Street. Incendiary bombs were rolling down the roads like moving soup tins. We worked right through the night on the fire until it was dowsed. I had about two hours sleep before going off to work.

Another night we were sent to the fire of Cartwright's timber yard. We worked close to a brick wall that collapsed during the fire. We learned later that two of the men from our section had been killed by the wall falling on them; if it had collapsed the other way it would have trapped us. What with air raids and spending time in our Anderson Shelter we seemed to be getting about two or three hours' rest every night.

On another occasion of our duty as fire officers at the B.S.A., the old buildings were bombed. They consisted of three floors of machinery: A, B, C and D sections set out as a rectangle with a yard in the centre. The bomb had almost demolished A, B and C sections and set D on fire. I was detailed together with Norman Winter to attend the top floor. Other teams were on lower floors. The fire was rapidly making progress between the ceiling and floor boards of the section above and because of heavy oil saturation the fire was intense. We had to try to remove floorboards in advance of the fire, and kept saturating them with hoses. We had four hoses at each level, one fixed on the gap, one under the floor, and we worked a hose each to douse the rest. The roof was collapsing as we worked and machinery ahead of us was crashing through to the floor below. It seemed an absolutely hopeless task. Overhead, belt-driven shafting and pulleys were crashing down as we worked. We reached the last escape staircase and Norman nipped off and left me on my own. I had moved well past the exit when I seemed to control the fire. The lower floors had been controlled at an earlier time. Finally, Norman having obtained help, a ladder was placed at the last window of the building and I was able to scramble out. We had saved about 30 feet of the building at each floor. I was pleased indeed to escape from that incident.

Shortly after we were married I was invited to be best man at a friend's wedding. The night before, the air raid sirens sounded but we were so exhausted we decided to stay in bed this once. A German bomber had struck the wires of the barrage balloon over Swanhurst Park and jettisoned his bombs. One of the bombs dropped between our house and a large bomb shelter in the field opposite. It was a personnel bomb, which on explosion set off a wide range of bomb splinters, used to do the most damage to soldiers as possible. Several of the splinters entered the bomb shelter and a woman and her son were both killed. The blast shattered all our windows at the front of the house and blasted the front door off its hinges.

At the impact Eileen jumped out of bed and passed out on the floor. Reaching over to help her, I felt a fierce sharp pinch on my cheek, and said to Eileen that a bomb splinter must have buried in my pillow, and just missed my head. There was hardly a mark on my cheek, and going back to investigate I saw in the light of the torch a hairpin on my pillow, which I had mistaken for a bomb splinter. We laughed a lot about this and it relieved the tensions. Examining the house in light of day we found a six-inch bomb splinter buried in the front room door. So it really was close. We boarded all the windows and rehinged the front door with the hinges in a different position. We were hailed as heroes at the wedding.

I was involved in two close calls on Home Guard patrol with Norman Crawford as we patrolled the factory. One night when we met at our respective checkpoints we noticed one of the firm's brand new B.S.A. motorcycles, and stood quite a while admiring the various points of the new model. We then parted and patrolled our particular sections. When we returned to our meeting place we found the motorcycle that Norman and I had admired had been the subject of a direct hit. The cycle was smashed into myriad pieces and the spot on which it stood was now a bomb crater. We contemplated on our nearness to oblivion.

On another patrol as we stood near our rendezvous

overlooking the canal and the playing fields in the middle of an air raid, we saw a house suddenly collapse before our eyes. It seemed as if the walls suddenly moved outwards and the roof of the house collapsed on the rubble. It was the first time either of us had witnessed a direct hit on an innocent household. Seconds after our awestruck sighting of the bomb we heard its explosion.

I had worked hard in the garden at Glen Rise and managed to plant essential vegetables like lettuce, radish and potatoes. Part of the garden had been a lime pit for the plastering for the whole of the road so we had a very well limed garden. It seemed with gardens that all I had to show was long digging sessions at 39 Brentford Road, at 83 Midhurst Road and now at 46 Glen Rise, a spate of continued digging. However, we did find the vegetables we produced worthwhile; they helped provide meals in difficult times.

With the collapse of the old buildings B.S.A. had to look for additional space. In winter we had arranged for machines to be available for our use at the Daimler factory in Coventry. My job was to arrange for the delivery of materials and for finished parts to be collected. Twelve turners from B.S.A. and one setter had to commute between the factories. I had to settle all differences. I was responsible for wages to the personnel.

After about three weeks of this arrangement we seemed to settle into a routine. Then Coventry was blitzed. We watched the waves of bombers and the flame-lit sky from the top of our shelter at Glen Rise. Next day I tried to get through, but roadblocks were set up all round the city. I got permission to visit the sites and report back. Both factories had been bombed and Coventry itself was flattened. I had a heck of a job because whole streets were closed by the demolition of houses, warehouses, factories and office blocks. I managed to salvage a few machined parts and returned to Small Heath. Mr Dickinson, the works manager, sent for me and took me to the bridge crossing the canal. We stood on the bridge overlooking the playing fields, large enough for three full-size football pitches; the whole area was completely filled with red rusty machines extracted from the fires. He said, 'That is the complete set of machines required to build our anti-tank guns, the Boyes rifles.' At Dunkirk, because of the weight, the anti-tank guns had all been abandoned on the beaches, and with the destruction of the barrel mill and C and D machine shops there was hardly an anti-tank gun in the country. 'Your job is to get those machines working and producing anti-tank guns absolutely as soon as possible. We have been allocated six factories in Mansfield. So sort out the personnel you require and get started.'

6

Mansfield

The first task was to get a full parts list, and quantities sorted out at the stores. Output of completed guns was always controlled by the number of barrels produced. So there were existing stocks of most items except the barrels. The tool room and outside sub-contractors were allocated barrel mill machines to get renovated first.

The second job was to sort out teams of operators who were prepared to move to Mansfield. Of all the operators required, only one barrel mill setter, one chambering personnel, one machine shop setter, two barrel mill operators and quite a host of multi-turning fitter operators volunteered.

The next job was to inspect and arrange allocation of production parts to the different factories. A visit to Mansfield was arranged with a full coachload of operators intending to transfer to Mansfield. I was in charge of the coach and had strict instructions to present a good impression at the factories we were being allocated to. No alcohol was to be consumed.

We set off from Small Heath in good spirits and in an orderly fashion. But it was not long before Murphy's law began to operate.

On the outskirts of Nottingham, three-quarters of the way there and right outside the pub known at the Blue Ball, the coach had a puncture. As in wartime the minimum equipment was carried, we had no tools and no spare wheel. Of course we pulled into the pub yard, and the boys rushed away to sup ale as if there was no tomorrow. We had to phone a Nottingham garage to send out jacks and a spare wheel; this seemed to take ages, and I resigned myself to a very difficult day. By the time we were mobile again the passengers were hopelessly drunk.

Circumstances could not have proved less favourable to our visit. We arrived at the first factory just as the midday break began and I appealed to the passengers to please behave themselves. But as hundreds of girls flocked out for their break, and while I was inside meeting factory officials, the passengers, as one, disembarked from the bus and stood against the nearest wall to urinate. From the window of the office where I was being received we overlooked this outrage. Words failed me, but the reception I received was to say the least cool.

On my return home my wife informed me we were to expect an addition to the family. So the first Sunday in January that I had free, we both travelled to Mansfield. The landlord of the local pub there told us of a bungalow to let; we immediately called there and settled a deal to take over the bungalow, 'Hilbrae', of Blythes Wood.

After this first sortie to Mansfield I still had a great deal to do in Birmingham to complete the renovation of the machines. So Eileen moved to Mansfield to settle in before I could join her. In the meantime two of my friends from the drawing office were told they were to work in Mansfield and asked if I could help find them accommodation. We arranged for them to be lodgers at 'Hilbrae' and look after Eileen until I could move up. I found a tenant for our house at Glen Rise, and having finalized my domestic arrangements applied all speed to getting our anti-tank guns ready for production as soon as possible.

At last the twelve boring machines were reconditioned

and available for transfer to Mansfield. I supervised their loading, taking every precaution to ensure their safe arrival, and motored up to Mansfield to supervise their transfer from the station to the factory for installation.

At Mansfield station when the train arrived I was flabbergasted to find that every standing leg of the lathes had been broken. In spite of every care the lathes arrived without a single leg intact. I supervised the unloading and delivery to the new factory at Quortex, previously engaged in the production of silk stockings. There we placed the boring machines in position and finding numerous tea chests available, set up the machine on top of the tea chests, concreted in position by filling each tea chest with cement.

I had one setter and recruited twelve girls used to making silk stockings to become boring machine operators under the control of the setter. We had received a full load of barrel forgings, and as soon as possible set up a centering machine to create a centre in each end of the forging. Working continuously, night and day, we managed within one week of occupation to start boring our first barrels.

The setter reported that his new girl operators seemed likely to equal any barrel mill operation he used to control.

While the boring mill progressed, machines were set up in the next section to work towards the production of a complete barrel. Rifling machines, reaming machines, spillbore machines, the complete machine for chambering, lathes and milling machines were installed and ready for production.

Rifling was a very skilled job. To put a greater spin on the bullet, so that it could drill through the steel plates of a tank, the rifling of an anti-tank gun had six complete spirals for each rifling groove. Girls that had been competent in findings snags or ladders in stockings were in fact ideal to train for this new mechanical refinement, despite the Small Heath experts who had denied the possibility of anybody other than fully trained skilled riflers being able to undertake this operation. We proved them wrong and the setter considered that his girls were as good if not better than the best operators he had in Birmingham.

We used to work all day, sleep upstairs on benches and start again at about 4.00 a.m.; sometimes I did not go home for four or five days in a row. The progress we were making was exciting and time-consuming. Then, just as the first batch of barrels were ready for chambering, the chambering operator fell ill and had to remain in bed. Everybody said that we could not carry out that operation without him. So we filled a van with a portable vice and holding device and transported the lot into his bedroom at his lodgings, much to the horror of his landlady. We fixed up the equipment by his bed, he talked us through the operations. In this way we laboriously built a first batch of 25 barrels.

Back at Quortex we hastened through the milling stage, to the final threading at the end of the barrel (to accept the flash shield). The machine for this thread milling was not yet complete, so we found a tool room and arranged for one of our operators to work all night and screw-thread the barrels on a centre lathe. We called next morning at about 6.00 a.m., and found that the operator, although he said he was a skilled turner, had screw-cut the barrels using a stock and die. We managed to salvage twelve barrels only.

There was no way we could progress without having the barrels proved in the soft stage and then hardened; for this they would have to be returned to Small Heath. On the Saturday night, when they were ready, we had the biggest fall of snow in March for about a hundred years. The AA reported that all roads out of Mansfield were closed. I loaded the guns and with one of the setters we set off at 7.00 a.m. from Mansfield, with sacking, shovels, pieces of plywood and lengths of chain. We virtually dug our way to Small Heath; some of the drifts were six feet deep. By using every means possible we managed to arrive at 6.00 p.m. We were expected, and operators were ready to work through the night processing the barrels which we were to collect at 8.00 a.m. on Monday morning. By then, snowploughs plus a thaw enabled us to return to Mansfield in two hours – the same journey that had taken us eleven hours the previous day.

When we started to assemble all the bits and pieces required we were short of a firing pin. We had all gauges and blanks ready but the special fixture had not been completed. We had a small Myford bench lathe so I set to work. It took me 78 blanks before I could finish 12 that met the gauge we already had at Mansfield.

So the first guns were built exactly six weeks after the old section had been wiped out. I received a personal telegram of congratulations from Lord Beaverbrook, the Minister of Supply at that time.

We continued to fit out all the other factories; I took over the Illingsworth factory. Mr Wood was appointed manager of the group.

Illingsworth was converted from a furniture manufacturers into the heat-treatment section of the group; we did production hardness testing and full inspection of the components before and after treatment. As I was spending long hours at work, Eileen was very bored and wanted to find a job. So I arranged for her to work as hardness tester, with a chair, because of her pregnancy.

Bill and Norman, our lodgers at 'Hilbrae', gave notice when Norman's wife, Massie came to Mansfield. We replaced them with Alf Davies, his wife and child. On our last weekend with Bill and Norman, we decided to have a slap-up Sunday lunch and kill one of the hens left in our care by the owner. We selected the hen, I found an old army cutlass, Bill held the fowl on the ground with its neck stretched and I raised the sword and struck off its head. The hen jumped up and ran round the garden without a head. I had planted rows of potatoes, onions and radishes; for this Sunday feast we dug up a few rows. The meal was superb.

Shortly after completing Illingsworth's contribution to the group, I was appointed to share control of another factory, Barringers, with George Johnson. We put on a night shift, because the components to be manufactured were getting in short supply. George and I shared day and night control on a monthly change-about. When I worked nights Eileen used the car in the day, and when she finished her day shift she woke me. We had a meal, and I took the car to work. We lived a Box and Cox life.

Eileen grew tired of sharing the bungalow with the Davies family, at about the time when she needed to give up work. So we moved to 26 Coronation Street and prepared for the new baby.

Massie, Norman Crawford's wife, decided to organize a weekly Friday night party, with a rota so we visited one another's house once a week. This one night out a week softened the pressure of hard work, though Eileen and I could only go when I worked on the day shift.

Production of assembled guns grew rapidly. We had now approached the time when all components had to be manufactured at Mansfield. I took over the Mansfield Shoe factory and installed machines and equipment to produce the components that needed large quantities in stock.

As Eileen's time drew nearer we had booked her in to the St Ann Maternity Hospital in Nottingham. Taking Eileeen to hospital, as she complained bitterly of her pains, I said to her, did she really want to go through with it? We both burst out laughing. Our daughter arrived at 4.00 p.m. on 17th September. She was christened Irene Ann, and this was about the only time she ever used her Christian name. As soon as she could talk, when she was scolded for being a naughty girl, she said, 'I'se not a naughty girl, I'se a naughty Bobbie.' From that time to the present day she has been known as Bobbie.

We kept up our regular Friday nights, though for a change we also alternated with the girls all going for a drink together and then all the men. Many of the times when the men were staying behind, I had to break off to change nappies or make a feed bottle.

7

Bristol

As manufacture of completed guns continued the stocks of the last items were being exhausted. The last dispersal factory to become available was Mansfield Shoe. So I was appointed superintendent of this unit and organized the installation and running of the last batch of machines and components necessary to complete the output of anti-tank Boyes guns.

At about this time an old colleague of my father, Mr Charlton of Austin, now a development manager at Bristol Aeroplane Company, asked Dad if he knew of a good toolmaker/development engineer. Dad knew I was getting restive at Mansfield and suggested Mr Charlton contact me. I visited Bristol and we both felt satisfied about the move. Mr Charlton then asked the Ministry of Labour to arrange my transfer. This went through and I was paid an accommodation allowance until I could find somewhere suitable to live.

I moved first into digs with Mr Charlton's assistant, then into a bed-and-breakfast boarding house at Henleaze: always scrambled egg paste for breakfast, and two rounds of bread to toast in front of my own fire for evening meal. I then heard of a family living at Long Compton who all worked at Patchway Bristol Engines, so in part exchange for bed and board I agreed to run them to work and back. This was a miserable existence. The water was drawn out of a well and it had all sorts of live algae swimming in it. All there was to do was go to the pub across the road.

Then by chance I heard of a bungalow at Pilning. Eileen came with me to look at it and we settled on moving to Dart's Bungalow, New Passage. The owners lived next door and together we were the only inhabitants of this isolated spot along the Severn Channel. The only access was 200 yards along the sea wall to the south of New Passage. We had to leave the car at the farm and wheel our shopping along the sea wall in a home-made box-cart. All the cooking was by primus stove and the heating by open fires. The bungalow was below the level of the sea wall and in times of strong winds and high tides the sea spray used to pass right over the bungalow into the back garden. Every four hours a manned anti-aircraft barrage station used to discharge a round of shells; the noise was deafening and shook the bungalow to its foundations. But my wife and daughter were with me and made it all worthwhile. Once Mum and Dad came over to stay a weekend with us. Dad said that I would have to find somewhere else to live; I couldn't expect Eileen and Bobbie to tolerate such conditions.

But Bobbie used to play happily with her imaginary family of children. One day she came with me to wheel the week's shopping back along the sea wall. The wind was blowing a gale and rain was absolutely stair-rodding down. I had a job to keep the cart on the sea wall. Bobbie kept crying and tugging at my trousers, screaming all the while. Nearly out of my wits, I found she wanted me to pick up one of her imaginary children and place her on the cart. Only then could we proceed; after I had picked up nothing and carefully placed nothing on the cart.

I also used to have evenings of skittles and joined the local pub team playing in a league against other local clubs, home and away. It was one of the few distractions in those days. Or

My wedding, 21st October, 1939

The winning team of the Bristol Aeroplane Company

Eileen and me at Newquay

Doug and me at Aberystwyth, Whitsun 1938

The building of our first house at Glen Rise, 1939

My first car

Our third car

Mum and Dad, Vic, Eileen and me, 1935

At Bournemouth: the last holiday of Vic with Sybil

Mum and Dad

Mum, Dad, Bobbie and me, 1940

My brother, Victor Sidney

Victor as captain of the King's Norton Secondary School cricket team, May 1935

Back-stand abrasive belt grinder

Assembly machine for Painton engine with raised assembly head

Assembly machine for Painton engine with raised assembly head showing movement mechanism

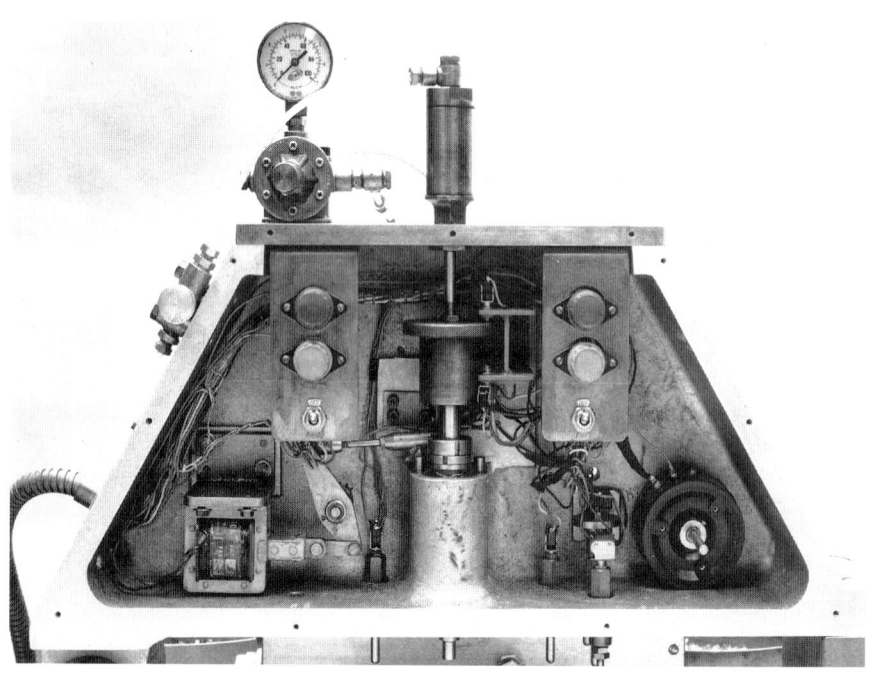

Assembly machine for Painton engine with raised assembly head view of open assembly head

Fixture for Rolls Royce

Another fixture for Rolls Royce

Multi drill head for Austin Motor

One of 50 exactly identical fixture for an automatic M/c Austin Motor

A special machine for Guest Kean

View of 12 special machines for Crane Seren

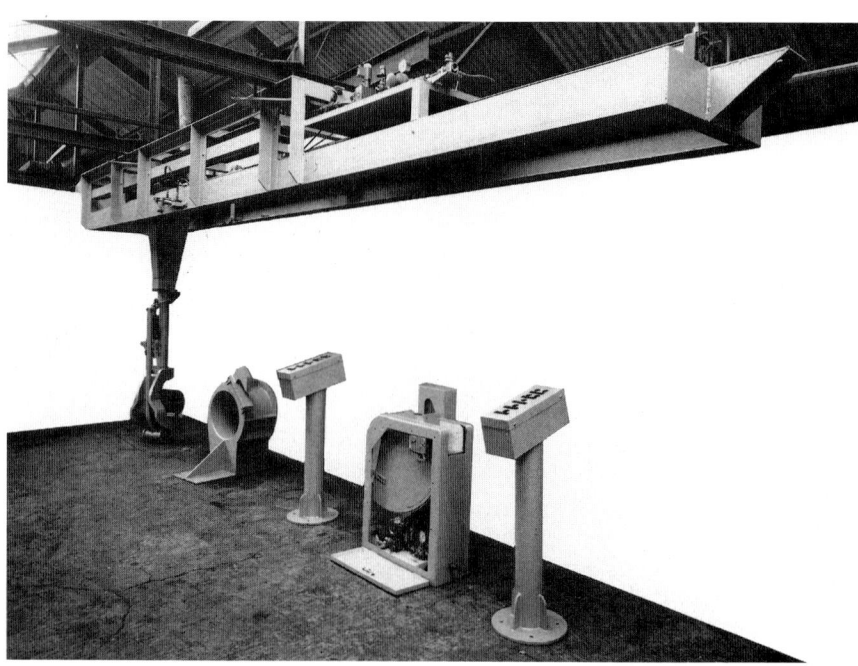

Photographs were not taken of the fabricated structure provided for the storage of steel bars manufactured by associate company Kheco nor of the duplicate cradle used to move the bar from the store to the cut off saw, nor of the timing and setting locking of the jaws of the cut off saw. All these were designed by associate company KHE Automation Developments.

Machine designed and made for multi drilling upside down for McLaren

Fixture for Coventry Radiator

Open view of special machine for Rubery Owen

Special machine developed for Birlec

Special machine developed for Richard Lloyd

Different attachments used on machine for Rubery Owen

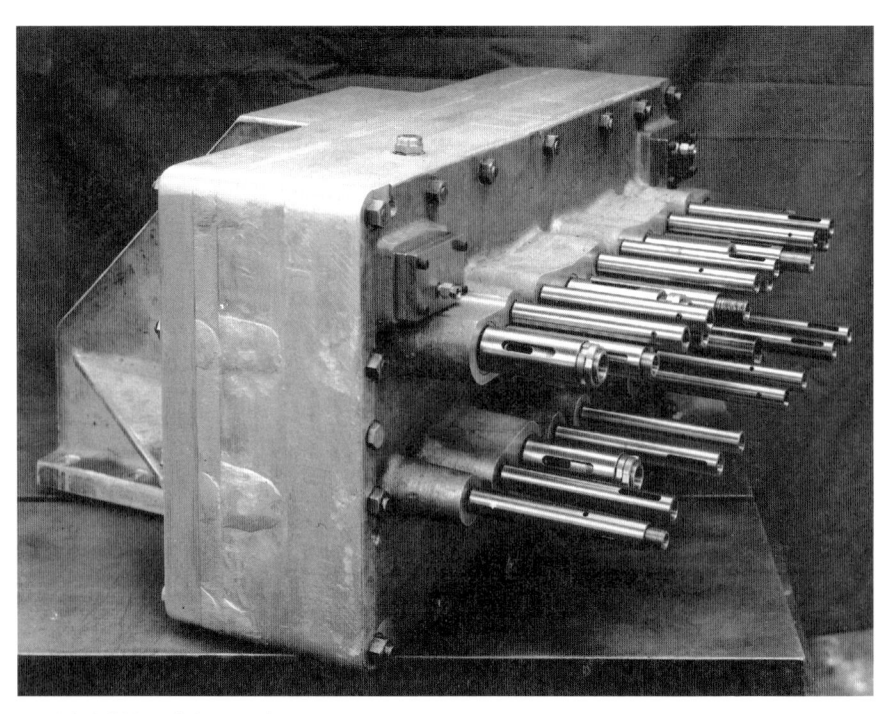

Multi drill head for Sankeys

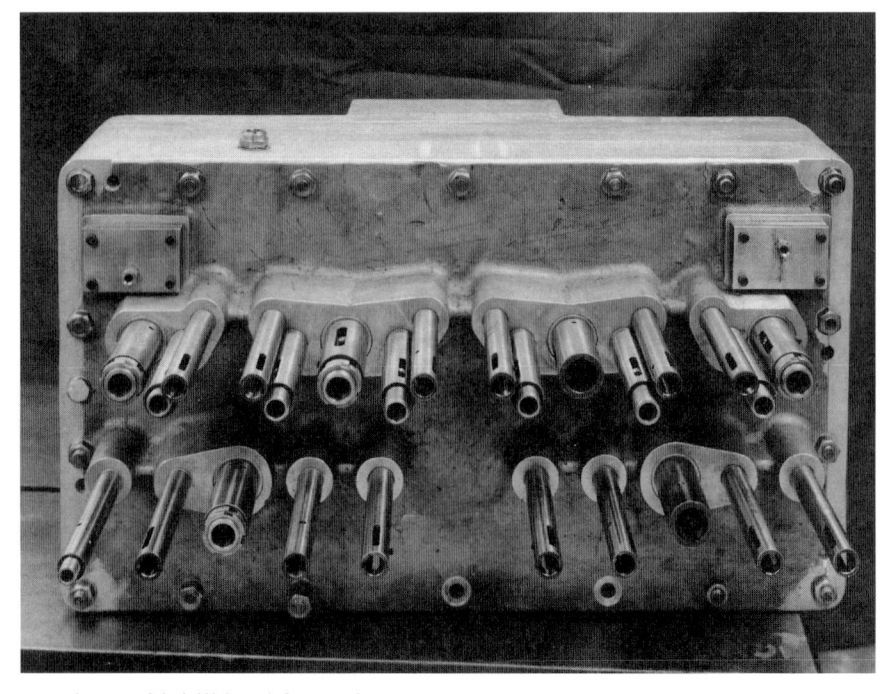

Another multi drill head for Sankeys

Special machine for Richard Lloyd

Reprinted from BRITISH ENGINEERING & TRANSPORT *June 1961*

Machine for cold rolling brake shoe blanks

PRODUCED by the King's Heath Engineering Group is a novel machine for cold-rolling brake shoe blanks from straight lengths of T-section steel. A British vehicle manufacturer was dissatisfied with the performance of foreign machines for performing this operation on shoe blanks for heavy vehicles; distortion of the rolled sections was necessitating a second machining operation. Technicians of the King's Heath Engineering Group, whose products include ring rollers, examined these machines, and then designed and built an entirely new hydraulically-operated machine, stated to be the first of its type designed in Britain.

Working under a pressure of 24 tons (24·4 metric tonnes) the rollers of the machine take a cold strip of heavy T-section steel and curve it in one movement to a predetermined size and shape, accurate in every dimension, without rippling of metal, distortion in curve or distortion in horizontal or vertical flatness, it is stated.

This it does at a production rate of 1,000 brake shoes an hour, which could be stepped up still further if automatic feeding apparatus were linked to the machine—a refinement which is already on the drawing-boards of KHE designers. Another unique feature of this machine is the needle-roller bearings on which the centre shaft runs, and which operate under conditions hitherto regarded as impossible, the hydraulic pressure on the shaft subjecting these bearings to a load of 50 tons (50·8 metric tonnes)

The KHE 904, as the machine is designated, is of surprisingly compact design being 6 ft 8 in (2·03 m) long by 5 ft 2 in (1·57 m) wide by 6 ft (1·83 m) high, is fully automatic, completely self-contained with automatic pressure lubrication from an oil reservoir, and requires only to be connected to an existing power supply. A battery of the machines could be sited in parallel in a very small factory bay.

Simplicity of operation and maintenance are also a tremendous advance on the existing foreign machines, it is claimed. To cite only one aspect: whereas the changing of formers for differing sizes and shapes of brake shoes on existing machines involves eight hours' work, the same operation can be carried out on the KHE 904 in eight minutes.

The machine has been ordered by other vehicle manufacturers, and engineers of many big transport undertakings and brake manufacturers have shown great interest.

This machine rolls a cold strip of heavy T-section steel into an accurate brake shoe blank at a high production rate

Brake show rolling machine

Brake show rolling machines

Brake show rolling machine

Assembly frames 24 off Brochurst engine

What No Bearing?

Not on the K.H.E. Hoverbelt Machine

Hoverbelt machine (patented)

Series of abrasive belt machines standard

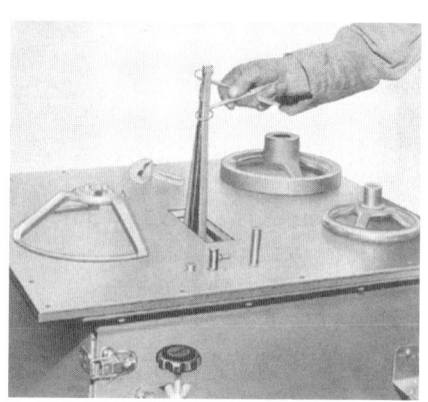

My family: Me, Bobbie, David, Eileen and Pat

Freeleen Cruiser

Special press for Lever Brothers

A report that appeared in a local newspaper

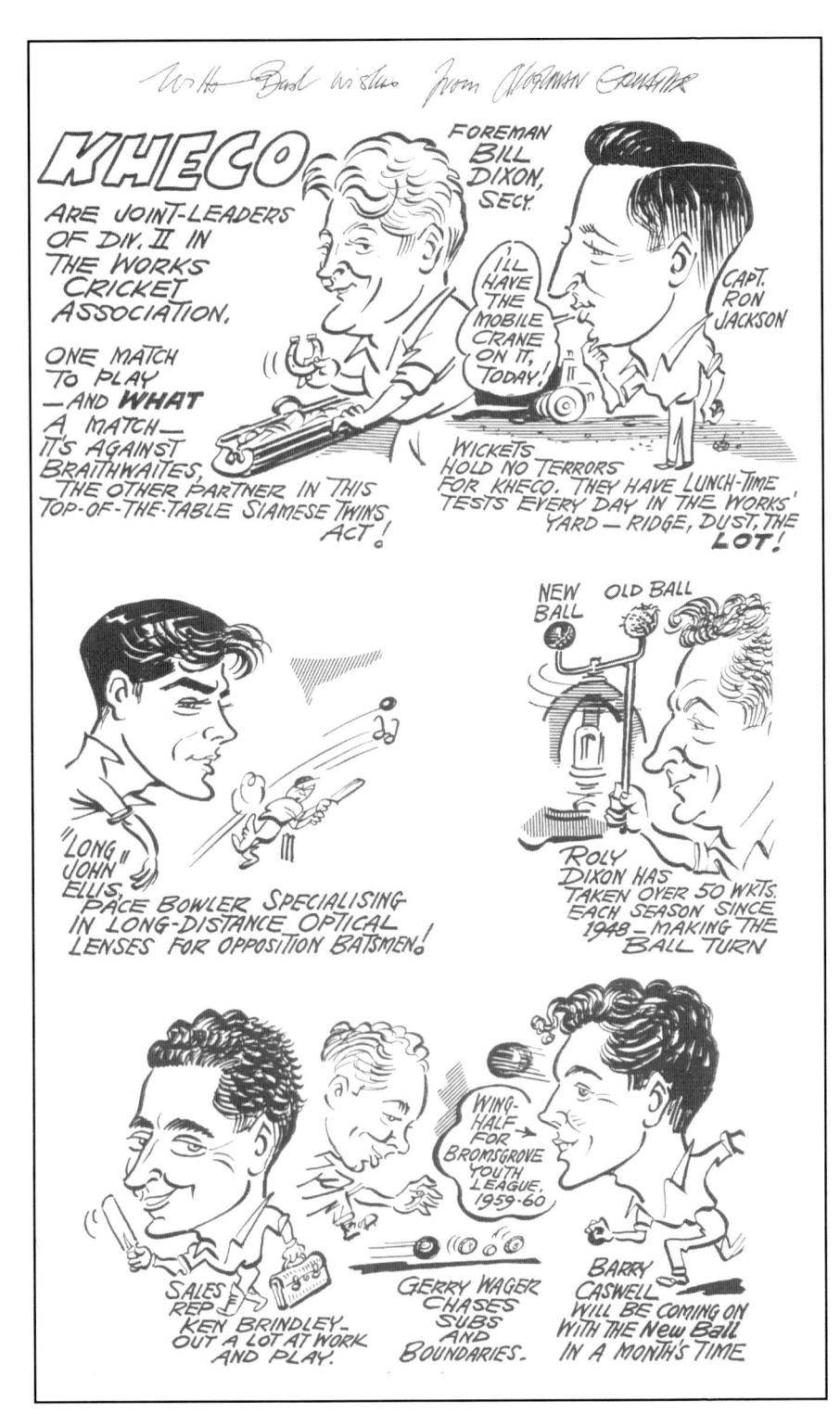

A cartoon which appeared in an issue of *Sports Argus* weekly paper

Presentation of trophies to section winners at annual christmas party, left to right: Ken Brindley (sales), Mrs Betty Stephens, Mr R. Stephens (Works Manager), Mother, author.

Weatheroak Ladies Night with my invited guests.

Queen Mum drops a line to local man

POPULAR Royals like the Queen Mother have met thousands of people during tours and presentations but not all are forgotten — as one Abergele man discovered recently.

Since he was presented to the Queen Mother in 1937, Mr. Fred Shelley, of 29 Bryn Twr, has always been one of her biggest fans.

So, on her 85th birthday, which she celebrated recently, he was among the thousands of people who sent her a card offering his best wishes and reminding her of their first meeting.

Last week, he received a letter from the Queen Mother, thanking him for the card and saying that she could remember their first meeting 'well, despite the time that had passed.

Answer

"I didn't really expect anything from the Queen Mother — after all, she could not possibly answer everybody who sent her a card. So it was a real surprise when I did get a reply," said Mr. Shelley who is an engineer. "I was presented to the Queen Mother and her husband, who had just become King of England, after being chosen as the apprentice of the year."

He added: "I was just a young man then, working at Austin Motors, Birmingham, and part of the prize was being presented to Royals at the Dorchester Hotel in London."

Mr. Shelley said the letter would be something he would treasure for years to come. "She is a very special lady," he said.

Mr. Fred Shelley at his Abergele home, with grandchildren Katherine and David, and his letter from the Queen Mother.

Council hope for the best

TODAY is the day that Abergele councillors hope will change the recreation facilities of the town for the better.

Members of the town council are appealing to local people to go along to the library today (Friday) to put their views forward about the recreational needs of the area to Miss Zena Wooldridge of the Loughborough Research team, who have been commissioned by Colwyn to carry out a survey into leisure facilities in the borough.

Coun. Mrs. Ruby Jones said: "It's the last chance to try and get amenities at Pentre Mawr, otherwise everything is going to go to Tir Prince at Towyn. We need as many people as possible to take part."

A report which appeared in a local Wales newspaper

sometimes Eileen and I used to drink a couple of cans of beer sitting on the sea wall and watching the sun go down over the distant Welsh hills.

The tide used to go miles out at low tide and there was a deep pool almost in the centre where we could swim and dive. It took about an hour to reach the pool, so we only had a little time before starting back, otherwise we would be cut off by the rapid rising of the tide.

One night a tragedy occurred right opposite the bungalow. Towards dawn we woke to loud engine noises and heard a tremendous bang. It transpired that a Flying Fortress returning from a bombing mission over Germany mistook the Severn Channel for a landing field, realized too late, jettisoned the bombs, tried to rev the engine and crashed in the sea. Three bodies were recovered the next day. The rest of the crew must have perished in the blast.

As winter drew near it became obvious that Eileen and Bobbie would have to leave to live with my folks in Guildford, and I would have to find other accommodation.

The reason Mr Charlton had needed a good tool engineer was to fit aluminium shields around the cylinder of the Hercules radial engines of the Blenheim fighters and bombers. It was found that in service the cast iron radial engines became red-hot and they were a clear target for German anti-aircraft crews. Because the engines had been designed so that every bit of space was utilised, the protective shields were of a very awkward shape and absolute precision was needed in creating the tools that formed the baffle plates. My job was to create these tools and then make sure they worked perfectly so that every plate fitted exactly in the small space available. Some of the designs of the tools were complex and needed extreme skill to produce components.

My office was a desk under the stairs of the Rodney production management team. I had a team of five fitters and a foreman, Ralph Parkes, to assist me. Ralph was a very strong man and a real character. He used to chew up razor blades, placing them in his mouth and crunching them up to small pieces. He used to open his mouth to show the bits of razor blade swimming in his saliva. He used to pretend to swallow them but I had a suspicion that he worked them under his tongue until he could dispose of them.

One day he saw two men loading sacks of shot-blast pebbles into a van. As he walked past he said, 'You don't need two of you to load those.' They said the sacks were over a hundredweight each. Ralph said, 'I will load those with my teeth,' and he did. He picked up the sack with his teeth and with hands behind his back go it swinging to and fro and then released it into the van.

Once when the works had just been painted and newly-painted steel girders left by the painters, he dipped his feet into a waste oil bin and walked up the girder, firmly planting dirty footprints all the way up to the rafters. He then took off his shoes, threw them down, climbed across the rafters and down another pillar. It was a huge joke to see the painters, when they saw the footprints going up but never returning.

One day one of the production superintendents bet Ralph that he could not throw a large weight 28 yards. Ralph accepted the challenge. At lunchtime the bet was set up and the tape laid out, while most of the lunchtime workers gathered to watch. Ralph threw the weight; it landed exactly on the 28-yard mark and he was paid his winnings. It transpired that if it had not hit the tape exactly, either before or after, he would have lost. This was the catch of the bet, which backfired.

We had just completed the tooling of the aluminium shields and passed them over to production when another crisis arrived. General Montgomery with the Eighth Army had just started to build up his El Alamein attack. The only planes allocated for desert warfare were the Beaufort and Beaufighter, built by the Bristo Aeroplane Company. When they were in service, it was discovered that desert sand mingling with the engine oil formed an abrasive compound so troublesome that a complete radial engine was useless after 90 hours flying.

There was an absolute panic at Bristol when the Air Ministry decreed that no Bristol planes could be supplied to the Eighth Army until fitted with an effective air filter. Apparently Vokes Cleaners had designed and had approved air filter assembly. A special meeting was called of all heads of departments in the British Aircraft Company. I was elected persona grata and I was given one month to produce all the tools, or create sub-standard cquipment so that 100 cleaners could be produced and a mass-production unit organized. It was a terrific task; each cleaner consisted of over 80 separate parts and over 1,000 tools needed to be produced in one month. I had full authority to claim any machine tool, or press or any workers required to help.

A few weeks earlier I had read in the press of a bungalow for sale at Yatton. Eileen told me that whatever it was, I was to get it, and then she would come over. So we sold our house at Glen Rise for the price of the bungalow at Yatton. As the property was empty we were able to move in right away.

I travelled back and forward to work by car using sidelights reduced to the size of a shilling and headlights with shuttered cones, just allowing a narrow deflected glimmer of light. I had to leave about 6.30 every morning. Because of the loneliness and the amount of time I was away, we bought a little dog to be company for Eileen and Bobbie.

From that time on several meetings were called for progress reports. Apparently the Air Ministry was putting pressure on Bristol and I suppose Montgomery was putting pressure on the Ministry. Anyway it all seemed to fall on my head. Because of meetings and continual interference the only progress we made was during evenings and nights. For a month I never went home. My wife caught the train in the evening to bring me fresh clothes and cakes she was able to bake. I had my clothes on most of the month, occasionally having a lie-down in the firm's surgery unit; having meals in the canteen and drinking gallons of tea. During the allotted time of one month we produced a full set of 'A' tools for the project, that is not hardened, and soft mild steel templates, hammer blocks and simple bending tools.

The fully designed and manufactured production tools took eight to ten weeks to produce in the tool room. We had to create quick, easy, hand-operated methods to produce initial components. The worst component was the scoop, which consisted of a panel about the shape of a kitchen washing up bowl but twice as deep. Special deep-drawing material was obtained but every time the depth of the stretch burst the component. For our first batch these had to be fabricated and welded together. In desperation, one day we tried stainless steel, the most brittle material possible, yet a perfect component was produced. Progress moved on until finally by fitting draw-heads, easing radii and controlling pressures with air cylinders we produced components from ordinary mild steel sheet. I was completely in charge of progress, and with tools being made in Bristol and all over the country, 'A' tools being built by another complete section and components produced by fitters and welders, I had a 24-hour job. I remember once scolding a machinist and falling asleep standing up against a pillar. During the later stages of the month we were all nearly exhausted. The longest stretch I did without a break was from 6.00 a.m. one morning, all day, all night, all the next day, all the next night until 10.00 a.m. on the third day, living on cups of tea and pieces of cake.

In the month allowed us, we produced 98 cleaners, a complete set of 'A' tools, and assembly fixtures made of wood, and laid out a production section for operation as better tools and supplies of components became available. Mr Wood was knighted, becoming Sir Stanley Wood.

Aircraft were being despatched to the Middle East. I had a long weekend at home and slept or rested from Friday night until I went back to work on Monday morning.

Soon after I was promoted to tool controller, in charge of all tool production, including the six dispersal factories' tool rooms, all tool purchasing, try-out, development, pattern shop and foundry. I was able to make the point to the management of the lack of machines and toolmakers at Rodney. Soon I had complete control to buy secondhand or new machine tools that were available, and enrolled over 100 extra toolmakers from all over the country. Rodney tool room was at last able to compete with the best.

I travelled all over the country to Air Ministry depots, stores or factories; also to check the progress of tools ordered from sub-contractors. One of my trips to London to visit sub-contractors occurred at the time the V1 and V2 robot bombs were targeted on London. Travelling on a bus down the Strand a doodlebug landed and shattered the glass windows in the back of the bus. Terrific damage had been caused to shops. Most of them were boarded up to prevent glass breakage but many people were injured and ambulances arrived. We all helped to move the debris to try and find out if anybody was buried. When all were accounted for the police and wardens dispersed us all.

Another time in London, having finished for the day, I decided to call on my parents in Guildford. Travelling down, a robot bomb fell in front of the train, wrecking the line and causing us to stop. We were all asked to wait in the train whilst a relief train was provided. As we sat waiting another bomb exploded at the rear of the train, so we could neither go forward or back. We all had to dismount and walk forward to the next station and wait for the relief train.

* * *

During my stay in Bristol I continued with my running and enrolled with both Bristol Athletics Club and Western Harriers. I was also selected to run the three miles at White City, representing Gloucestershire in the All Counties Championships. I finished seventh. Earlier I had won the West of England (which included Devon, Cornwall, Somerset, Dorset and Gloucester) half-mile and one-mile scratch race competitions.

My time for the mile was 4 minutes 26 seconds. Sydney Woodeson held the World Record for the time of the mile in 4 minutes 13 seconds. My time for the half-mile was 2 minutes $\frac{1}{2}$ second. The extra $\frac{1}{2}$ second prevented me from being presented with a standard trophy.

In my last year at Bristol, I tried to win the Victor Ludorum Trophy. I won the mile and ran the half-mile in the Open Medley for Bristol A.C. against the best teams in the South of England. A team of Jamaicans attached to the Air Force were favourites. I ran the half-mile first and handed over the baton in a dead heat position and we went on to win the relay. Our photograph was in the Bristol Aeroplane Sports Pavilion for years. This race was brought forward, as many of the teams had to catch trains. It spoilt my performance in the half-mile; I only finished fourth, so I lost the trophy. When I left Bristol and they asked me what I would like as a leaving present, I said I would like a replica of the Victor Ludorum Trophy, which was a model of the Blenheim bomber. So instead of only holding the trophy for one year, I now have one for keeps.

I also became involved in the social club and became chairman of the supervisory social section. Other members of the committee played golf and we set up a regular golf game on Sundays at Hanbury Golf Club. Because of petrol shortages I used to catch the milk train at Yatton at about 6.15 a.m., ride with my cycle from the van at Temple Meads, cycle up from Temple Meads across the downs through Westbury up to the Golf Club. I used to be able to leave my small bag of clubs with the pro. Sometimes my pals had teed off and I joined them on the second hole. We just had time to finish the round and I had to cycle back to Temple Meads to catch the 12.30 train. If I missed the midday train the next was at 6.00 p.m.; so sometimes I used to cycle all the way home to Yatton.

On Saturdays whenever possible Eileen and Bobbie used to catch the train to Bristol. I would be working until 6.00 p.m., when we would meet at a café, have tea and toasted teacakes, go to the pictures, call for a drink at a pub, and then drive home. On one such outing Bobbie wandered off and we lost her. After spending hours searching for her we found her at the police station, chatting away to all the police force. After that she was a little devil, always trying to get herself lost so she could go back to the police station. Years afterwards she wanted to become a policewoman, probably because of her experience.

The war with Germany came to an end in the summer of 1945. All sorts of street celebrations were held. A gang of us from the works travelled in a car with a sunshine roof, and I remember sitting on the roof with my legs in front of the windscreen with one of the girls from the office as we drove down to the Central. Everybody was dancing and cheering. Six years had taken a toll on our endurance; everybody relaxed and nonsense prevailed.

We went to Guildford for Christmas in 1945. Dad had been very poorly and had been home from work; the doctor said rest would help him recover. Over the holiday Dad suggested we set up a toolmaking business of our own. He thought he had enough contracts to provide orders and I could look after the manufacture. We decided that as the war with Germany was now over there would be a demand for tooling expertise.

The gauge and toolmakers were holding an exhibition at Earl's Court and in conjunction with my job I arranged to visit London on Friday, 23rd January, giving me time to have a weekend in Guildford and return on the Monday morning. I had a most terrible attack of the 'flu; headache, coughing and sneezing, and I nearly cancelled the trip. However, I went, toured the exhibition and caught the train home to Guildford. By this time I was nearly a hospital case. I phoned the works on Monday, having decided to stay another day at Guildford. Dad returned to work on the Monday and that evening attended a meeting of the artisan section of the Merrow Golf Club. He came home upset and went to bed early, shouting down to Mum, 'Are you coming up, Ede?' Those were his last words. He passed away in his sleep. The next days were hectic, trying to arrange everything. Mother was absolutely stunned; she kept shouting upstairs, 'Come on, Alf, get up.'

They had been living in a house provided by his firm, their house in Southam Road, Birmingham having been sublet. After the funeral in Birmingham we managed with great difficulty to get Mother to drive back to Yatton in Dad's car. On that day we had the thickest fog imaginable. I still had a terrible cold, and with the weather so bad, windows down, and having to keep getting out to find our whereabouts, it took us most of the day to arrive home.

But Mother wanted to return to Birmingham.

8

King's Heath Engineering – Beginnings

There was no doubt that Dad's death created a great change in my fortunes. Leaving Bristol and friends was a wrench. I had become involved in a responsible job and was chairman of the supervisory social section, and we had a circle of friends. It was very hard to hand in my notice. The management at Rodney were very kind and tried their best to induce me to stay, even to the extent of allowing me a month off to put my affairs in order and settle my mother in Birmingham. However, after a family discussion, the best course seemed to be to leave Bristol and return to Birmingham.

Mother stayed with us at Yatton whilst I served my month's notice. I advertised the sale of the house at Yatton and the sale of Dad's car at the same time. Events moved at a rapid pace, and by the time I had worked out my notice at Bristol, the house was sold, the furniture loaded on a van and we all set off for Birmingham, sorry to leave Yatton and the Bristol area.

My parents had let their house in Southam Road while they were living in Guildford; we made the tenants an offer of £100 and their departure was arranged.

On returning to Birmingham from Bristol my mother received a deputation from Dad's friends. Dad had confided to them that he had wanted to initiate me into his Masonic Lodge. He had always had hopes of me one day becoming a member of Francis Davies Lodge, and they wanted to know what Mother thought of the suggestion. When Mother later asked me what I thought, I said that if that was Dad's wish I would be interested. Accordingly an appointment was made for me to meet a committee of past masters of the Francis Davies Lodge. I answered all their questions to their satisfaction, and was asked to supply two non-Masonic and two Masonic references. At the October meeting in 1946 I was initiated on the same Bible presented to my Dad on his initiation. At the festive board after the meeting the Bible was circulated round the dining room and all the officers, members and guests signed their names on the flyleaf. At the very next meeting of the Lodge in November I was asked to act as steward, and from that November I was never out of office until I resigned in 1973. I received my second Degree in March 1947 and my third in October of that year. I regularly attended the Lodge of Instruction under the Banner of Masefield, the Mother Lodge of Francis Davies Lodge. I was able to perform various offices in the training classes and was congratulated as a good ritualist and a worthy successor to my father. Eileen and Mother joined me at each Ladies' Night.

During my period at Rodney, I had a number of dealings with Sheridan Precision Tools. They had completed a good many tools on a short delivery for the Vokes cleaner project. During the visits paid by their managing director, Mr Pinnock, I had established a good rapport with him. On one of his visits he told me of the problems caused by shortage of management, and many times offered me the job of manager.

On returning to Birmingham I called on Sheridan Tools and told them of my circumstances. They immediately offered me the job of works manager. So within one week of leaving Bristol I was in employment, and within a few days of joining I was complimented by the chief salesman, who said 'At last there is someone in charge who knows what toolmaking is all about.'

The company worked to a Jewish system; a late meeting every Friday night, Saturday a day off and Sunday a normal working day. At one of the Friday meetings I queried the output target set for the tool room. Examining the figures I found a number of names of workers not under my authority, and later found that they had left the company. Their wages were still being drawn, and added to the output target calculations.

On another occasion, one Saturday when the works were closed, I called in for some estimates I had prepared. I heard voices in the turning section and as I quietly approached heard Mr Pinnock inquiring of the shop foreman what he thought of me. This did not improve my opinion of the company, and I felt under scrutiny.

Finally, at one of the Friday meetings, I expressed my concern about the people on the payroll having wages drawn on their behalf. I was told it was no concern of mine. I protested that it was my concern and that these wages should not be included in the output target I was expected to produce. This incident led to me parting company with the firm.

During my stay with Sheridan Tools I had had close contact with a Bill Green of W.G. Green Co. Ltd. Sheridan Tools had carried out many machining operations for him. On hearing of my severance with Sheridan Tools he offered me a directorship with his company, which I accepted. I was to take charge of the toolmaking side of his firm. However, I was not happy with this new company; its capacity was very limited and it only employed two toolmakers. Nevertheless it led to me meeting the two Biggs brothers, at whose suggestion I thought of starting my own business. This was an idea I had previously discussed with Dad during my last visit at Christmas. He had said that he could get all the orders we would require, and I could run the manufacture side. Dad's solicitor, Mr Mills, greatly assisted me in making the arrangements to set up on my own. He registered the company in the name of Shelldon Precision Tools; Mother and my Aunt Vin agreed to become my partners and we paid the initial £100 formation fee in July 1946.

I started in the garden shed at Southam Road, with Fred Woodward as the first employee. We started on a Ten X Rifle order, which Bill Green had agreed should be transferred to us. During my time at Sheridan Tools I had dealings with the local machine tool supplier, and from him I obtained a lathe containing special accessories that enabled cutters to be held in the chuck and milling operations carried out. Fred was a very good salesman and made a lot of contacts for orders, and suppliers of steel, which was in short supply. I worked in the shed on the lathe and together we managed to make a small profit that paid our wages.

One day I was travelling on the tram to town when I noticed our former Mansfield tenant, Alf Davies, sitting nearby. He said that he was now works manager of a local firm, King's Heath Engineering Company. They were engaged on a contract for Remington Rand which they were unable to complete, and he did not know what the firm intended to do. I told him about setting up on my own in business and Alf said that the firm would probably be prepared to rent out part of their premises. I left him with my telephone number. Some time later he phoned me to say that he had fixed a meeting for me with the managing director.

At the meeting I was offered a small part of the premises for a rent of £3 per week. The complete works consisted of a two-storey building with a lean-to. There was a wooden store shed, and a lean-to built of breeze blocks with a corrugated iron roof. The machine tools consisted of a large shaper in one corner of the lean-to, a power guillotine, a couple of fly presses and two small power presses. On the lower floor there were three old capstans and four small horizontal milling machines, all belt-driven from an overhead gantry.

Upstairs was a small partitioned-off tool stores and drawing office. The premises had a lease until the year 2006.

Mr Hunter explained that the other directors would be prepared to sell their equity. We finally bought them out on 30th September, 1946, and commenced trading as King's heath Engineering on 1st November. We invited my mother and auntie to become directors on investing £1000 each and I then started to purchase surplus machine tools from the Ministry of Supply depot, used during the war in munitions factories. We bought a lathe for £270, a vertical miller for £100, which we converted to a jog borer, a band saw, radial drill, fly presses, capstans and a universal grinder. We then obtained two sets of slip gauges plus a surface plate, giving us a fairly comprehensive tool room unit. We also recruited many employees from Sheridan Precision Tools and had a labour force of twenty toolmakers, fitters and machinists. At the end of October Ralph Parkes joined the company as works manager, and persuaded a top-class toolmaker, Ivor Latcham, to join us.

Ralph lodged with Mother and Aunt Vin. He would have liked to have joined the company as a director, but I said it was better to wait until he found a place to live in Birmingham. We looked at several properties but none were suitable. Then Eileen, fed up with being at Southam Road, said if we could afford to buy Ralph a house why not one for us? Accordingly we looked round and finished by buying 36 Falstaff Road in Shirley, conveniently near to Southam Road and King's Heath Engineering. At last we became a complete family again at Shirley. Every time I returned home from work, my daughter, Bobbie, would grab me before I removed my coat and rock and roll with me before I could relax.

On other occasions, my other daughter, Pat, would jump on the arm of the fireside chair just as I arrived home and collapsed in the chair between 7 and 8 p.m. in the evening.

Eileen scolded her and said, 'Let your Dad rest a few minutes, he has just returned from work.'

Pat would then place her legs across mine and appeal, 'Play Incey Wincey Spider, Daddy.'

I had to walk my fingers up her leg saying, 'Incey Wincey Spider, up the spout he came. Down came the rain and washed the spider out' and I had to brush my hand down her leg then say, 'out came the sun and dried up all the rain. Incey Wincey Spider up the spout again.'

Then she would say, 'Change spouts, Daddy!' and I had to repeat this on the other leg.

Eileen would then say, 'Pat let your Dad drink his tea,' and, after a repeat performance, Pat would jump off the chair and go to bed.

Shortly after Ralph had to move back to Bristol to help his brother in his timber business. At about this time Mother considered moving to North Wales and I helped her purchase a bungalow there. Since nothing could persuade Ralph to stay with us, it was then that Ray Windwood was appointed works manager in his place.

Soon we were a competitive tooling company and were able to obtain contracts from Richard Lloyd, Austin Motors and Bristol Aeroplane. I made several visits to Parker, Winder and Achurch to try and find a market for piercing pliers, but they were difficult to work effectively, and finally we came to the conclusion that it would be better to write the whole consignment off as a bad job. However, the buyer of Parker Winder and Achurch said there would be a small market for electric fires that were stable, conformed to electric standards and were reasonable in price. So I returned to the works, designed a pair of castellated side plates, obtained samples for the assembly and we set about producing our first electric fire. We registered it as a Shelldon product; the name was a combination of Shelley and Dixon. The first six fires, built in my office after works closing time, were fully approved, and orders of 20 per time were set up for each month with P.W.A. The fires were a two-bar design with a side switch to control one bar. This was just a spare-time activity, and I assembled all the fires we made in my office when everybody had gone home. On occasions Eileen came back with me after tea and helped assemble the fires, so apart from materials very little cost was involved.

One day a representative called; he had seen the fires at P.W.A. and asked us for a comprehensive contract. He was an exporter of refrigerators, and thought that the fires could, with the right packaging, be placed in the compartment of the refrigerators to save separate shipping costs. He thought his customers would be pleased with the fires, and asked for 20 fires to test the arrangement. He would provide the packing. He drew a large wad of £20 notes from his pocket and paid in advance for 20 fires, saying his requirement would be for 200 fires per month. Suddenly, we seemed to have had some good fortune. Sure enough, when he collected the first 20 he said he would send a van to collect the next 200 as soon as they were ready, and pay in cash for this first order. All future sales to be on a monthly credit basis. We agreed to this arrangement.

I enrolled members of the family to help on evening shifts to assist in the assembly. I paid everybody out of petty cash at £2 per hour and classed the expense as part-time wages. When the 200 fires were completed we phoned for the van to collect. It happened I was out on business when it called. The office allowed the fires to go, although I had stressed that delivery would depend on payment first. The driver conned the office girls that he would post payment off the next day.

A series of phone calls and visits produced no response. Sure enough we had been swindled, and although we engaged debt collectors and agents they reported that they had tried in vain to obtain settlements from this man, for other firms, without success.

One day we saw one of our fires for sale at Rich and Pattison and on enquiring found that they had bought the full delivery for cash from our mysterious buyer. We finally had to write off the project as a bad job.

However, Fred Woodward, our first employee, had done a great job on supplies and deliveries. He had found suppliers for the aluminium castings and electric components and had even organized a die-casting company prepared to produce the die-cast tools for a very reasonable sum. He had also found a company prepared to buy the complete fires, and all the spare components we had in the stores.

At about this time we were able to negotiate more orders from Austin Motor Company for jigs, tools and press tools manufacture, and we managed to get a foot in the door of the buying office for the supply of production-machined components. Further contacts with P.W.A. led to supplying special door locks for the Middle East. They needed the key to rotate twice to lock and unlock. Yale Company had been approached, but because of the difference from standard building requirements, would not undertake to retool for this special requirement. So it was back to the drawing board to design a two-throw lock. The letter of credit which was shown to me was for the supply of 50 different key combinations and was worth £25,000, deposited with P.W.A. This job required considerable tooling, forgings, springs, brass castings and other materials. To get the project moving we spent over £1,500 on the tooling and raw materials. The first 50 samples were produced, dispatched and approved. During the first week of production suddenly out of a clear blue sky the Middle East changed their currency from Sterling to Francs and we had one month before the letter of credit was revoked. All we were able to complete in that time, working flat out with a temporary night shift and employing all my uncles and friends under temporary labour charges, was £500-worth of finished sets of locks. We had spent over £2,500 in producing this final quantity of 100 sets of differing keyholes before the letter of credit expired. We were left with thousands of part-completed locks, plus the full quantity of production items which were useless for the home market because of the two-throw condition of the locks. We finally had to dispose of the locks, the piercing pliers and all the left-over components of the Remington Rand filing system. This completely cleared out the old shed that we had christened North Works.

The buyer of P.W.A. was very concerned about our loss on the lock contract and gave us an order to produce ball catches to be used on prefabricated houses being built in Australia. I designed a ball catch and patented it under the name of Shelldon, and a set of die-cast tools to produce the body. As in all the production contracts Ivor Latcham manufactured all the tooling required. We were producing ball catches at about 1,000 per week. P.W.A. then became worried as we had over-supplied their original order and other sales outlets seemed limited. We had to close down production to low key. We obtained production orders for components from Austin Outwork Production Department which just about salvaged the production department.

We engaged an inspector, who held quality control qualifications. At about this time we were looking for a good local hardening firm and my cousin had just started a new heat treatment firm in Sparkhill. We had orders for a gearbox lever used in the Austin Princess car and we were working to a good schedule. Part of the component needed to be case-hardened at the working end of the lever. We entrusted this operation on the component to this new firm. Suddenly there was a panic because Austin discovered that the case-hardening had been too deep and the working end of the lever broke off in operation. Austin had to withdraw all Princess models sold and replace this lever. This of course caused the Austin buying office to lose faith in our reliability. So through no fault on our part we lost considerable orders.

We had also produced a series of different sized gearbox units for the standard-range cars. Suddenly the schedule was reduced and we found these orders had been transferred to Cleveland Autos in Somerset.

Meanwhile our buildings began to require considerable maintenance. We found that a serious leak had developed in the roof and needed urgent repairs. We obtained the materials for the roof repairs, as well as timber for benches and all our requirements in sand, glass, cement and timber. We had a supply of bricks delivered by the London Brick Company. We built a cycle shed and incorporated it in the building of the outside wall. Because we had difficulty in closing the premises securely, we fabricated a pair of iron gates and gradually replaced our broken fencing with brick walls. Two colleagues and myself would lay 500 bricks of an evening after finishing a day's work; this stopped the losses we had suffered from vandals, and children turning on the taps of the oil barrels. We stored steel stocks in the North Works, but rain pouring through the wooden slats in the roof had caused deterioration of materials. One Saturday I decided to re-lay the roof with mineral felt and re-tar it completely. Setting up an empty oil drum with a stock of tar and a fire underneath, and borrowing a ladle, brush and tackle, I set about repairing and re-tarring the roof. I was part way through when a chap called up to me on the roof asking if I knew if a job was available at the works. I asked him his trade and he replied 'An engine fitter.' I said there might be a chance and to enquire at the office. He asked what the boss was like, and I said 'Oh, he's a proper bastard,' and continued tarring the roof. A long while later I was called down to see the works manager; he thought I ought to meet someone that could be useful to us. I was introduced to the chap who had asked about a job. I don't know who was most embarrassed, me in my old clothes and reeking of tar, or the chap who recognized me as the workman on the roof. Anyway he was offered a job and worked for us for many years.

There came a time when we needed to organize a proper grinding section for we now possessed an internal, an external, two surface grinders and a profile grinder. So at the time that a full two weeks' holiday was given, the last week in July and the first week in August, four of us set about the task of replacing the wooden shed of North Works with a proper brick-built unit, 60 yards long by 10 yards wide. As the works left on Friday afternoon we commenced dismantling the timber structure. All materials had been ordered and supplied. It was late Saturday night before we mixed the concrete for the stanchion bases. It was so dark that we had to feel the concrete by hand to check its density. We worked through every day until dusk, and finally all was finished except for painting. We did just start to emulsion paint the brickwork before we packed up, absolutely whacked. But the building was finished and ready for occupation. The workers on their return could not believe that we had managed the alteration on our own. The grinders were moved into position the first working day back, but it was some time later that the painting was finished.

We arranged with our printers to produce a presentable apprentice certificate and we made arrangements with the Lord Mayor's secretary that our successful apprentices would have their certificates presented and signed by the Lord Mayor in his Parlour. This arrangement continued for many years.

Ray Windwood, our new works manager, suggested that we might be interested in producing cycle hubs. His brother James Winwood had developed a new type of cycle hub. Apparently one of the problems of racing cycles was spoke breakage. This was a development following the lightening of the cycle frame, causing a weakness in the wheels and the large hubs favoured by the racing fraternity. The side to side oscillation of the pedals, with the tyres and rims of the wheels being held by the road surface, caused the spokes to break. Normally the spokes were bent at 90 degrees, inserted in the hub flange and then strained back to lace through the rim. This meant that the spoke head was forced to an angle very much in excess of 90 degrees and therefore subject to fracture. James had developed a hub with an angle on the flange resembling a flat disk with upturned sides. It enabled the spoke head to remain less than a right angle and permitted the spokes to be laced in a parallel line – less of a strain on the spoke head, and the spokes being set at parallel tension meant spoke breakage was eliminated. We made all the tests necessary to prove the idea had possibilities and organised a manufacturing programme. We then patented the idea, had leaflets printed and booked advertisements in the cycling journals. We also managed to get a good recommendation and write-up by one of the Midland specialists in the racing field. At about this time a local toolmaking firm transferred their total capacity over to producing a large flange hub, but instead of the usual ball and cone bearing they used a ball race fitted into the hub. This was highly successful, but spoke breakage was greater with a large flange hub. They approached us to see if we could combine the two developments, but we declined. We understood from making various enquiries that the cycle racing fraternity preferred to keep to the individual method of adjusting their own cone tensions.

When the Olympics were held in London in 1948 I went to Windsor Park where all the cycling events were held. I called in at the cycling competitors' training quarters and left leaflets about the hubs. We received many export orders as a result, and many local suppliers started to stock our hub. One local racing cycle builder fitted our hubs to all his models. One day we received from Australia an order for enough

TRADE NEWS ...

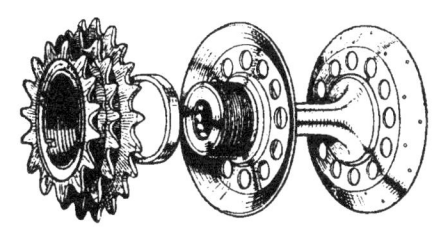

INTRODUCTIONS AND DEVELOPMENTS FROM THE MANUFACTURERS

LIGHTWEIGHT HUB

In designing its new Shellwin lightweight hub, the King's Heath Engineering Co., Ltd (Kingsway Works, Moseley Street, Birmingham, 14) has aimed at reducing the risk of spoke breakages, and for this reason the flanges on the hub incorporate a change of angle so that the spokes retain their natural line and the heads of the spokes are not placed under undue strain. The design, it is claimed, also produces a more rigid flange. Use of larger diameter cone locking nuts is also made to prevent the "pulling over" of the wheel, the large, flat surface of the nut giving a good grip on the frame slots. Spacing washers of varying thicknesses are supplied with the hubs so that the wheel can be adjusted initially to give the correct chain line for any proprietary derailleur gear and to give the correct central position for the wheel in any frame. The weight of the hubs, minus sprockets, are: Rear $7\frac{7}{8}$ oz.; front, 7 oz., and the prices are: Standard front hub: 33s. 6d.; standard rear hub, 36s. 6d.; derailleur rear hub, 37s. 6d.; double-sprint rear hub, 38s 6d.; double-sided rear hub (derailleur and single sprockets), 39s. 6d. All cups and cones are made to standard sizes and $\frac{1}{4}$-in. diameter balls are used in both front and rear hubs.

hubs to fill a tea chest. We completed the order, cleared all the paperwork and sealed the box. The consignment had to be on a boat leaving London Docks on Boxing Day, which meant we had to get the box to the docks by Christmas Eve. There was a dock strike at the time, and when I arrived at the dock gates, there was about a three-mile queue of lorries in each direction. So I parked the van in a back street and carried the case of hubs to the gate. The dock guard said all the lorries were waiting to unload for the same vessel that I wanted, but having assured the officer that I could get the case on the boat myself he allowed me through and gave me directions to the ship's moorings. There was no one there to sign for acceptance, so I climbed the long, long stairway and after many stops I reached the deck of the ship. A ship's officer on duty signed for my consignment, led me to the hold and directed me where to place the tea chest. If I had waited for clearance through the proper channels I should have waited at London Docks for about three weeks.

We had many follow-up orders from Australia and New Zealand, and delivered tea chests of hubs to all the principal ports in the UK.

Suddenly we started to get rejections and returns which began to escalate the costs. Apparently our old machines were beginning to show their age and accuracy was deteriorating. It meant replacing all the capstans at an estimated £2,000, or give up the project. Reluctantly we decided on the latter course.

Now that Mother was happily living with Aunt Vin in Wales, she said that I could have Southam Road on condition I kept a separate bedroom for her and Vin to visit Birmingham whenever they liked. But Eileen had reservations against moving back to Southam Road because it was too dark and too old-fashioned.

Dick Smith and Bill Moran from work helped me transform the house. There was a dining room with a step down into the kitchen, another step down into an outside toilet and a coal house. I knocked the lot down and extended the dining room and kitchen to include everything out to the original building line. The kitchen was then fully equipped with everything modern, a stainless steel sink with electric waste disposal, a dishwasher, washing machine, and so on. I then remodelled the dining room and built a patio with three french windows to look out over the garden. I next opened up the hall, knocked down the old enclosed stairs and replaced them with an open staircase built on steel girders. In fact I did anything that Eileen wanted, paid out of my loan account at the firm. Finally I was able to purchase the other half of the semi-detached house next door and join them together in a single unit.

At about this time Rose Poole, the wife of Harry, our transport manager, asked for a change of job from capstan operator. When I offered her the job of nursemaid to my children and helping Eileen with the housework she jumped at it.

After we had moved to Southam Road and Rose had become part of our house and one of the family, Eileen developed a wonderful lifestyle, divided between bridge, housework, bridge and shopping. We had a happy family life because of our love and our affection for our three wonderful children. Their happiness made all our problems recede to nothingness. My main sadness was that because of my commitment to my job I had missed Bobbie's formative years.

Pat was a beautiful baby, and she won several baby beauty shows, but there was a time when we nearly collapsed with exhaustion. She developed a mastoid in her ear and for fully six months we had little rest. Eileen and I had to work an alternate shift programme between 6 p.m. and 6 a.m. On Eileen's evening rest period, because of the noise Pat made, she used to go to the local cinema, pay for a seat near the wall and sleep until she was awakened to go home. She never once saw the film but said it was well worth it. How Pat could keep screaming all day and night was a mystery. But suddenly during Eileen's turn on duty the mastoid burst, and we all had peace at last.

David was a very obedient child, protected and shielded by his elder sisters who did not want to see him punished. Everything he broke or did wrong was done in the cause of a scientific experiment.

We all settled in at Southam Road.

One day at the works, Rose, wife of the Transport Manager Harry Poole, came to me and asked to be taken off the capstan machine she had been working on and asked if there was anything else she could do. I asked her if she fancied helping my wife look after the children and doing a bit of housework at my home. She jumped at the chance and said she knew all my children and would love to do that. I agreed to pay her the same wage as she was getting. So Harry ran her to my house at 7 o'clock every morning and Rose made breakfast for us all, saw the children off to school and helped with the housework.

It was only when I returned to Birmingham that I was again interested in the Blues and their fortunes. During the later part of the War, apparently a small fire had been started in the west stand for the purpose of training the fire squad of the ground staff. It got out of hand and burnt the complete stand down to the ground. Season tickets were then put on offer for seats in the temporary stand for £100 and I bought one and at last had a comfortable view of the match.

Later I purchased two season tickets with the idea of taking Eileen or one of the children with me, just as my Dad had done with me. The children expected me to give them sixpence as an incentive to come with me. They spent it on sweets and when they were eaten they wanted to go home. On Saturday nights when I went to the newsagents for the *Sports Argus* and the children came with me it used to cost me about ten shillings for a threepenny paper.

In the 1960s I used to plan business trips away to coincide with the Blues' fixture list. I would call on customers in that area of a Friday night, stay the night, see the game of a Saturday afternoon and travel home after the match.

Because of the two season tickets, I could obtain stand tickets for Blues away games in a Cup tie. Eileen really used to enjoy those matches. Harry Poole would bring Rose over in the van in the morning to look after the children, then he would drive us to New Street Station down the central road in the Jag. We would get out and the football special was about twenty yards away. He would then pick us up at night from the same spot on our return. As soon as the train left the station drinks were served and sometimes there was a dining car and we would eat and drink till we reached the match venue. We would then shop around for some gifts to take home for the children. On the return home, drinks would again be served as soon as the train left the station.

Eileen very much enjoyed the Cup tie with York City. Because it was a long way we started early and arranged the usual drill with Harry and Rose Poole and, when the train left the platform, drinks were served. We arrived at York and the only tie cancelled that day was the match with York City. So we crossed over the bridge, boarded the train, and after a short wait we set off on the return, the bar again being open as soon as we left the platform. Eileen said that was the best match ever.

In 1965 Birmingham was drawn away in every Cup tie, winning every match, and we saw all of them. They were through to the final to play Manchester City at Wembley. I had a regular annual bet with the local bookie and, because most of my workforce placed regular bets with him, he gave me odds of 50 to 1 on Birmingham winning a Cup Final. I placed a bet of £20 on a win every year.

The night before the match I had a dream that just before half-time, with the score 1–1, Birmingham right winger

Gordon Astle shot a ball from close to the touchline, exactly in line with my view. The ball flew into the top right corner of the goal and in my dream Birmingham won three goals to one.

On the train on the way to Wembley we were offered £100 for each of our stand tickets, but I was too excited to consider any offer. I was going to see Birmingham make history, win the Cup, and I would win £1,000. The match went strictly according to my dream, with Manchester scoring first and Birmingham equalising and, just a few minutes from half-time, sure enough Gordon Astle sent a shot towards goal exactly in line from my seat in the stands. It made my dream feel so real, for I could not have known where I would be sitting nor which way they would be playing. As soon as the ball left Gordon's foot I was on my feet with my hands in the air, shouting at the top of my voice, 'GOAL!'. One hundred thousand spectators and Birmingham's goalkeeper Gill Merrick must have heard me. The ball passed inches from the top far corner of the goal. I bought the 16mm film of the game and the actual goal was very very close to the goal in my dream. My shout was not on the recording but I bet half the ground heard my outburst.

Whenever Eileen came with me to a football match all she watched was Gill Merrick and she used to feel sorry for him if the play was at the other end of the field. She used to say why couldn't they have another ball and let the players in defence have shots at him to keep him warm!

I remember the Cup match at Carlisle that Birmingham drew after being three down, and the river at the rear of the Birmingham goal was overflowing on to the pitch in the second half. Gill was standing in about 4 inches of water and the flood waters were slowly rising. Eileen wanted the trainer to take Gill a pair of Wellington boots to save him from getting pneumonia.

Eddie Brown was one of my favourites. I saw him score

direct from a corner kick and shake hands with the corner flag. Another time he collided with a policeman over the touchline and shook hands with him before going back on to the field of play. Another time he was playing on a very wet pitch and as he slid down after some tackle, he pretended he was rowing a boat and bent down over his toes, stretching out him arms and pulling back as if he were rowing back and forth in the Boat Race for all he was worth.

One year I sent a photograph of my daughter Pat to the Blues supporters club in answer to their appeal for applications for the competition for Blues Girl of the Year. She attended all the qualifying heats, won the competition, and was presented with the title, a case of champagne and two season tickets. They wanted her to go on to the finals of all the Midlands clubs and then on to the national finals, but she declined. She only attended the Blues competition because of me.

9

Industrial Relations and Machines

One Saturday morning a young lad walked into the office and asked for a job as a draughtsman. I said the only way he could get drawing office experience was to sign on as an apprentice and part of his training could be in the drawing office. He agreed and I passed him over to the works manager, who put him through several practical tests. Later he reported that the lad was equal to apprentices already engaged, and suggested we give him a trial. So he was offered a job and he started on the next Monday morning. His name was Jeffrey Rooker. His career was closely monitored. He worked on all the machines in the tool room for a short spell and finished as a fitter on the bench. He attended college on day release and his reports were so good that he was transferred to the drawing office. At one of our monthly production meetings his future was considered and all department heads submitted their reports on his progress. It was agreed to send him to Aston University. We were closely associated with the university and offered practical training to many of the students they recommended as worthy of encouragement. We told the university that whatever programme they thought would benefit Rooker we would pay costs and allow him extra day release. On completion of his apprenticeship he was granted a certificate, presented to him by the Lord Mayor of Birmingham. (He is now Lord Rooker and sits in the House of Lords.)

Later Jeff asked to see me and said he would like to leave and join the Navy as an artificer. I persuaded him that his record and achievements in engineering could provide him with a better future, and also explained that we had spent a lot of money on his education and expected him to stay with us at least a full year. He did, worked very hard and repaid our support. So at the end of the year his request to leave was granted. Later we heard that he had entered politics and had become the MP for Aston Brookfields.

We only had one strike in the whole of our business activity. We had introduced a production bonus scheme based on time taken on an operation against the time estimated. We had recently engaged a toolmaker who turned out to be a strong active union member and tried to involve the workforce in joining his union, without success. The local trade union branch who had also tried to interest the workers in joining a union saw this as an opportunity to get a foot in the door with this new recruit. To try and prove the value of union membership he decided to object to the bonus scheme, and asked me to withdraw it. I asked him for time to consider, whereupon he immediately registered failure to agree and said the whole company was on strike until such time as a suitable alternative be accepted by the workforce. This was about 10.30 in the morning. Everybody stood about in groups and many of the old employees said to me they were sorry to see this state of affairs. I phoned the local pub, the Station Hotel, and asked the manager to open up for us and supply drinks as to a private party. I then proposed to everybody over the loudspeaker system that we all retire to the Station Hotel. This suggestion was accepted and we all filed into the back snug bar. As soon as the bar opened I announced that I would settle the account. When everybody had been served, I went from table to table and collected all the grievances. At 2 p.m. the landlord called time and I said to everybody, 'Let's get back to work.' Everyone returned; I paid the bill. Back at work I put up a notice calling for the creation of a works committee to meet management once a month to air all disputes and grievances. The first agenda was posted, which included all the complaints collected at the pub and asked for three nominations from the workforce. The union representative made sure he was included on the list. In spite of repeated efforts by the union man everyone carried on with their jobs and added two further names to the list of committee men. Some time later we gave the union man a job he could not do properly so he was given his cards. The chief union convener called on me and claimed unfair dismissal and discrimination against trade unionism. I said 'Prove it. Everybody is happy back at work.' We never had any further complaints and the works committee sorted out the bonus figures to everybody's satisfaction. This was the only industrial action we suffered in 24 years.

Whenever the men worked overtime, Harry Poole, our transport manager, used to call at the local florist, with whom we had a monthly account, and take home to the worker's family a bunch of flowers. All the wives said, 'Thank you, I guess my husband is working late for Fred Shelley.'

At the annual company dinner, prizes were distributed for ladies' and gentlemen's tennis, fishing and darts competitions. At this function I tried to dance with all employees' wives. They all used to say to me, 'No way will I let my husband leave you. I shall stop that.'

During our years in business we organized a weekend in Blackpool to see the illuminations, paid for by the company, and on the 21st year arranged a trip to Rhyl, in three coaches, to the Queen's Hotel.

We had bought a steel trailer for use with our eight-hundredweight van; it was useful in collecting steel bars and steel plates and also in the delivery of finished tools and products, such as the large pieces of equipment and press tools we built for the Austin Motor Company. One of these tools was over two tons and no one would take the responsibility of driving it in the van and trailer. So I agreed to drive the van on my own to Longbridge, a journey which included descending a steep hill with a canal at the bottom. In spite of every precaution the van careered to the bottom of the hill, mounted the pavement and clattered along the railings on the canal side of the pavement. If I had crashed into the canal with that load on top of me, my fate would have been sealed. Finally, however, I reached the Austin works, where I had to cross the double tramlines of Bristol Road to enter. Traffic was dense; it was near lunchtime with queues of trams in both directions and queues of people waiting for the trams. As I crossed the lines, with one bounce the large tool slid out of the trailer and landed in the centre of both lines. Nothing could pass. Luckily I spotted a fork-lift truck in the works forecourt. The driver heard the commotion and was persuaded to come to the rescue.

We were always in trouble with lifting problems owing to the low roof in the main machine shop. We obtained a three-wheel donkey device which helped lift heavy machine parts onto the various machine tables, and helped assembly of large tools. When we saw a gantry for sale to anybody that would dismantle it and transport it away, we paid £18 for it and erected it outside the West Works. The uprights were strongly cemented in position and when set we organized the lifting of the cross girder about 20 feet in the air. While I was fixing the overhead crossbar to the vertical uprights I fell from the ladder. The boys swore that an indent which appeared in the concrete yard after my fall was the mark of my teeth.

Shortly after we purchased a second-hand swinging jib crane which could lift between two and six tons according to the jib angle. We cemented a reinforced base and built two side stay girders and fixed them at right angles to one another straddling the West Works.

At about this time we read of a garage with three petrol storage tanks for sale, free delivery, so we added an extension to the office blocks to hold these three tanks, filling them with diesel oil. We also installed five heating units in the works; working conditions were greatly improved. We rebuilt the toilets and installed better washing facilities. Finally, to complete the building programme, we built the drawing office in the spacious yard.

We received an order from a firm in Southampton that presented us with a problem. They had made all the designs for a machine tool to produce motor car gaskets. It consisted of a large table with a series of tools fastened on the circumference. Each tool carried out a specified operation on the gasket. We had built all the tools and each performed a specific operation perfectly, but when the complete assembly was set in motion it worked perfectly twenty times and on the twenty-first the locking plunger failed to enter the locating bush. If this happened on production, all the tools would be smashed. We studied this problem for a long time. Meanwhile the firm in Southampton were anxious to obtain their equipment but I insisted that the machine could not be sent until we had cured this problem. The cause was that a small difference in alignment built up, which the plunger could correct, but as each time this increment gradually increased, at the twenty-first time the plunger failed to engage. When we received an ultimatum from the customer I insisted that designers, fitters and management returned that night and worked through until we solved the problem.

The shop labourer, Bill Forster, had fetched us all fish and chips, the fellows' wives had been told and received the usual bunch of flowers. All the drawings were spread out and everybody contributed their opinions. During the night Bill came to me and said, 'What's the trouble, guv'nor?' I explained that the table overran every so often and we were trying to stop it. Bill said, 'You know those capstans that I have to clear out the swarf from? I like to hear the operator – when he winds the big handle back it goes CLUNK.' I could have shouted 'Eureka!' We designed an inner ring with five slots in it and a tapered plunger so that any slight inaccuracy would be corrected before the outside locator operated. The equipment was made, hardened and ground during the night and when assembled the machine worked perfectly every time. We were able to deliver the equipment the following day and the company were delighted. I arranged for Bill to have a £50 bonus for his suggestion. He could not have been more pleased if he had won the pools.

We advertised for an estimator to improve our quotations and balance our costing. Sid Styles applied for the vacancy, was accepted and after a short time extended his activity to sales. It was mainly through his activities that the company expanded, an expansion that cost a great deal of money before we established the right set-up. We started by acquiring for rent premises in York Road. We moved all the presses and the welding equipment there. This new development helped us to expand our activities to quote for larger welding projects and flame-cutting for industries.

We then received a letter from a Mr Gish of Caterpillar Tractors asking us for details of our capacity. We made an appointment and I travelled to Glasgow to the temporary headquarters of the American parent company. Mr Gish was an American sent over to establish a Scottish plant. He said that if we created a drawing office with 8 foot by 6 foot drawing boards, we would be considered for part of a gigantic development. On my return I organized the delivery of six large and four smaller boards.

There was insufficient room at the Kingsway works for a drawing office, so we looked for premises nearby. Two doors away we found an office block and stores with two separate floors above. The rent was nominal provided we undertook to repair the floors and brickwork. Meanwhile we advertised for and engaged some very good draughtsmen, had the drawing boards delivered and set up a new company called King's Heath Engineering Automation Developments (K.H.E.A.D.).

We started to receive orders from the Scottish-based American company for design work. Before we returned the drawings we quoted for their manufacture. This way we increased our turnover. We engaged a Scottish representative on a commission basis. I was appointed director of King's heath Patternmakers Company, who manufactured all our patterns, but now we had priority of service. Sid Styles set up a sales office and appointed a sales representative in South Wales, who was also the representative of the National Union of Manufacturers for South Wales, so he was in the area.

I was on the committees of the N.U.M. and the E.I.A. (Engineering Industries Association). I later became Chairman of them both. In my capacity as chairman I had a great deal to do with the secretary of the N.U.M., who was in close contact with the planning department of Birmingham City Council and kept me informed of likely developments and premises that were becoming available. Later he decided to leave N.U.M. and set up on his own with two other partners, and invited me to become a director. They proposed to take over a company of toolmakers and work for us as sub-contractors. The new company was registered as H.B.S.R. The S stood for Shelley. We arranged to transfer some work to them and also gave them an order to recondition three of our old milling machines.

Sid Styles introduced me to Modern Tool Designs at Coventry and I became director of that company. We were able to offload a great deal of design work onto them. I also became a director of S.R.K. – again the S stood for Shelley. It meant that we had, in all the companies together, a total labour force of 120 toolmakers, 36 designers and over 150 operatives. We also established a production unit in Garrison Lane to carry out mass production on automatics and capstans. They produced all the inner parts for the Shellwin cycle hub.

We established a social sports club with tennis courts, a snooker table and dart board, and Highfield Football Club joined as associate members. A tombola sweepstake was organized with the profit being under the control of the sports club committee. All employees of the various companies with which we were associated were elected members of the K.H.E. sports club. We played knockout competitions in tennis, snooker and darts and formed an angling section. As president of the sports club I obtained a stretch of water at Pensham and we had exclusive rights. We entered the Sports Argus Trophy and reached the semi-final twice.

Because of the great deal of travelling I was doing I bought a second-hand Jaguar car, had it reconditioned and sprayed black. I tried to plan business trips away to coincide with the Birmingham City Football Club fixture list. I used to call on customers in that area of a Friday, stay the night, see the game on a Saturday afternoon and travel home after the match.

Eileen particularly wanted her own car to go where and when she liked. So one Christmas in the 1960s I decided to buy her an Austin Mini, and planned it as a surprise. Since Mother's garage at Southam Road was in urgent need of repair I also decided to get that complete before Christmas and secrete the Mini there.

A week before Christmas we all moved down to Southam Road and to prepare the decorations, Christmas tree and festoon the hall with coloured lights and trimmings. I was on duty for Christmas midnight mass at Shirley Church on Christmas Eve. I drove there in the Jaguar and after the service changed it for the Mini. I then had to drive the Mini into Mother's garage and close the doors. I had previously devised a treasure hunt and laid all the clues with the last one to involve a search in the newly-constructed garage. I had put presents for everybody on the seat of the Mini.

Eileen next morning could scarcely believe that her present was her own car. The same Christmas I got an Austin pedal car for David, who was six years old. Later when I exchanged my Jaguar for a new automatic, David said, 'I don't know what Dad is bragging about – I've had a two-pedal car for ages.'

10

Caravans and Boats

I suppose the first interest we had in caravans was aroused by my visit to Dennis Bros in Guildford. The tool buyer manager told me of an old gypsy caravan he was trying to sell for £100. I mentioned this to Mother, and she asked me to buy it and take it to North Wales for her. So I paid for the caravan on my next visit to Guildford. It was in a back garden deep among overgrown plants and shrubbery, untouched for many years. Eileen's brother Len had come with me to help; together we cleared away years of undergrowth. Fortunately, we had allowed a full weekend to get the caravan back to Birmingham. We blew up the tyres, hitched it to the van and slowly set off. After about 50 miles one of the caravan wheels collapsed. We had to manoeuvre through a gate into a field, remove the caravan wheel and return to Birmingham in the van. We managed to buy a new tyre, return on Sunday morning, fix on the wheel and complete the mission.

Mother and Aunt Vin then visited Prestatyn to find a site. A few days later they phoned us to say that Winkup's camp would offer one, but their office closed at 9.00 p.m. and we had to be there before closing.

I left the works at 5.30 p.m. and by the time we were ready to leave it was after 6.00. What a journey it turned out to be. The caravan was very heavy and the Sunbeam not up to towing up a steep hill. We had to make several stops before reaching Ruthin. it was well after 9.00 p.m. when we phoned Winkup's, and there was no reply. When we finally reached the campsite there was no one about to show us where to park the caravan. At a point in the road there was a grass reservation so I towed the caravan onto it and set up the jacks. My hands were covered in grease. I connected up the caravan to the battery on the car to obtain lights in the caravan, but they did not come on. I then connected up the cylinder of calor gas – still nothing. By now it was pitch dark, and several interested campers stood and watched my performance. Eileen had fixed up the children on the top bunks. Eventually I went to sleep fully clothed, with hands filthy with grease, unable to wash because of no calor gas or electricity. What an introduction to caravanning.

Next morning Mother and Aunt Vin arrived and we found our allocated berth and rechecked the connections and lights. After a few adjustments all was working successfully.

Mother had met a Mr Gardiner who built 30-foot long caravans if the buyer supplied the chassis, complete with towing brackets, jacks and brake connections. After seeing his caravans, complete with all internal fittings, kitchen layout and sleeping set-up, Mother ordered two. I made several measurements and returned to the works. We managed to obtain various parts from scrap vehicles, built two complete chassis and delivered them to Mr Gardiner at Stoke. He built the two caravans in one month and delivered them to Winkup's camp at Towyn for us. The following year Mother started to hire the new caravans to holiday makers while living in the gypsy caravan. Mr Winkup helped Mother to obtain a lot of bookings.

Following the success of Mother's venture, I decided to purchase a caravan built by Gardiner, so I manufactured another chassis and delivered it to Stoke. Meanwhile, Eileen's brother Cecil was driving to Cornwall on business; we asked him to look out for a caravan site for us. He found a site on a camp at Hayle, and when Mr Gardiner had finished the caravan we towed it down to Cornwall for a week's holiday. Later we had purchased a Dovedale caravan and when friends came down with us they always stayed in that. We adopted a regular pattern for holidays; a week at Easter to open the vans and reinstall them on their site and a week in September to pack them up and move them to their winter store.

In time we began to build up a regular rental agreement with several families. To expand the site we purchased a second-hand Coventry Knight and two Bluebird caravans and fixed up our private area. We installed television sets in each of the caravans and in order to obtain a good reception built a large telescopic mast, 90 feet high. The aerial had to be lowered at the end of the season and re-erected at the start; most years I had this job to do on my own or with the help of the family.

The caravans were registered as a business venture under the name of Cornish Riviera Holiday Caravans and the letting business progressed very well. We were taking bookings for about 16 weeks of the year, which allowed us to invest in better facilities, every year providing newer caravans and equipment.

During our many visits to the caravans at Hayle we often went to Falmouth and became very friendly with Joe and May Seyfert. We went on many fishing trips with them and helped Joe with his boat. I also served as mate to him on trips with visitors to the Scilly Isles and around the Cornish coast. Joe eventually persuaded me to buy a boat of my own. I submitted an offer for an ex-naval harbour launch with a copper-sheathed hull, my bid was accepted and I went to Swansea harbour where the boat was moored. The boat seemed very sound. On making enquiries I found its maiden voyage had been as part of the flotilla of small boats which went to Dunkirk to rescue troops. It had been destined for duty in the Indian Ocean.

The size of the boat was convenient to build on a cabin superstructure, so arrangements were made to deliver it to a boat builder at Mylor, near Falmouth. We had the forward cabin built with a seat each side, hinged so as to form four bunks. The centre section had a toilet and cupboard for storing clothes; the main cabin midships was a galley with a seat which converted to a double bed. There were electric lights, a fridge, radio and television. When the boat was completed and Joe saw it for the first time he said, 'It's like a bloody caravan.' We christened her *Freeleen*, and we had many a happy holiday aboard her.

Joe subsequently persuaded me to buy two more naval launches when they became available, which we named *Joleen* and *Mayleen*. We registered them with the Falmouth authorities and set up the 'Cornish Riviera Boat Hire Services'. We arranged for World Holidays Afloat to organize bookings for us on a commission basis. A friend of Joe's, Derek, was appointed our representative at Falmouth. We limited the bookings to people who were either naval personnel or had had experience of handling boats on the inland waterways. We built up a regular clientele that booked year after year. The business prospered and we covered the original outlay many times over.

After a time the family decided that the *Freeleen* was moored too far away for them to enjoy as often as they wished. We decided to leave the *Mayleen* and *Joleen* at Penryn for bookings and look for a mooring for *Freeleen* nearer home. I made a visit to Wroxham one weekend and arranged for a mooring there, and plans were made to sail *Freeleen* from Falmouth to Chichester in the first leg and to Wroxham for the second leg. We set off from Falmouth at high tide early one morning, planning to reach Torbay on the first day, Poole Harbour on the second and Chichester on the third. On the second day, just off the Portland Point, the engine cut out and we rapidly drifted out to sea. Before we lost sight of land I signalled a Mayday call. Meanwhile the mate I had with me discovered that the fuel supply pipe had sheared off into the tank of diesel. We were able to start the engine again by ladling out diesel from the tank using the teapot. The Poole lifeboat reached us just as we got under way again. From Chichester we took the boat on to the Norfolk Broads, where we could use it more often, arranging the journey for a school holiday. The first stop was Newhaven, the next Ramsgate, where we were not allowed into the inner harbour which was reserved for permanent berth holders. We had to moor in the outer harbour which had a tide difference of 20 feet – stories were told of boats being moored and finishing hanging on the sea wall by their mooring ropes at low tide. We were able to moor alongside a barge, slept aboard the boat and set off early next morning for the final leg of our journey to Wroxham. As we reached the North Sea just past the Sovereign lightship the wind suddenly grew in intensity and reached gale force 10. I had to steer the boat bow first into the waves and use the trough to set course due North. It was a frightening experience for at the crest of the wave the propeller was threshing in fresh air and as the boat slid down the wave it bit into the water and the speed of the boat increased towards the very base of the next wave, the crest of which seemed a mountain above us while we were diving towards the sea bed... It only took a few seconds before the full sequence repeated itself and it seemed to continue for an eternity. The crew were very seasick and were rolling about the floor of the cabin in agony. I was at the helm of the boat continuously for 14 hours without a break. By steering as far west as I was able at the base of each wave we sighted land at Aldeburgh. We had a 4-foot depth of hull and constantly watched the recordings of the radar depth gauge, for with heavy seas the waves bouncing on the sea bottom would cause us to capsize. We passed the mouth of the River Blythe at Southwold, then on past Lowestoft and finally reach sight of Yarmouth. Here we had to moor against the harbour wall and await the visit of Custom and Excise officials. At high tide we passed through the lock gates from the harbour into the River Bure and to our journey's end at Wroxham.

We were able to spend very many weekends aboard the *Freeleen* and had more pleasure and enjoyment out of the boat than at any other time. We spent long weekends at Wroxham and enjoyed fishing and relaxing there, away from the problems at work. We had many trips from Wroxham down the River Bure and up the River Yare to Eccles and Norwich and found many pleasant restaurants and pubs.

We then sold the *Mayleen* and *Joleen* crafts.

11

King's Heath Engineering – Expansion

During one of my many visits chasing orders for work I met Mr Johnson, of Sankeys, who was responsible for research and development of their projects. We manufactured a considerable number of multi-drill units for various sizes of wheels produced by Sankeys; in fact, we built a good reputation for design and quality of the equipment we produced. Mr Johnson was a fine gentleman, straightforward and honest in all his dealings. After one of his visits to Germany he came back with an idea for the first operation of rolling steel sheet for producing car wheels. He sketched a rough plan of a machine he had seen for us to design a workable machine layout for him. We designed a high quality set of straightening rolls and a flying guillotine that could be adjusted for different circumferences of the various-sized wheels. The clipped sheet was fed into a rolling machine built on an angle, in order for the sheet to be accepted by the first roller of the machine, which had three upper and two lower rollers, each adjustable to any size of wheel.

The machine we produced gained much acclaim, and visitors to Sankeys when shown it were impressed. Rubery Owen ordered three sets of fully attenuated lines for their wheel section and we had orders from Dunlop and Pressed Steel of Coventry. We had developed the equipment to start from a 4-foot-diameter roll of material, fed through straightening rollers, cut to lengths by the flying guillotine, through the rolling machine into a welding mechanism that joined the ends of the circular component, then into a surfing machine that removed excess weld from top and bottom of the faces, then into a machine with formed rollers that produced a complete car wheel. Our customers were delighted with the accuracy and speed with which the wheels were being automatically produced. We were given a glowing write-up in the *Machinist*, from which we received many enquiries, some from abroad.

We were introduced to Maurice Clews, a member of the management at Sankeys. My family and I spent time at Wellington with the Clews, and they visited us at Southam Road.

Our families became close friends and holidayed together in Cornwall. I introduced Maurice to golf and arranged tuition and games for him; he became an addict. It was a sad day when, playing the game he had grown to enjoy, Maurice died on the golf course as he played a shot out of the bunker at the twelfth hole on the Castle Bromwich golf course.

We had an order to design and manufacture equipment for Richard Lloyd, who asked us to design and build a machine fixture to be attached to a milling machine, which would mill the slots in a turned blank to accept the cutter blades. The slots had to be varied in size and in the angle across the blank, because of the finished cutter being used on different materials. As well, the equipment had to be adjustable for different sized blanks and different numbers of slots in the cutter blanks. When complete, this equipment was sent to Tenbury Wells, one of Richard Lloyd's dispersal factories. The fixture performed exceedingly well and we were congratulated on our ingenuity and workmanship.

We tackled a similar problem when making equipment for Vickers. This time the fixture was to produce bevel gears in different sizes and different numbers of teeth. Again the customer was very satisfied with our efforts.

We purchased a profile milling machine from Cincinnati. It was a wonderful piece of plant. It accurately produced an exact shape from a pattern or a set of form plates or gauges. On one of its copying functions it produced a very tiny line, visible across the work piece. When the plaster pattern was examined we discovered a hairline crack which had been picked up by the machine. We also had orders for jigs fixtures and machined components from Cincinnati.

We produced a special plastic moulding machine for Birleg which was to be connected to a generator producing very high voltage, 10,000 volts. After delivery we attended the installation and try-out of the equipment, because we had no way of proving the machine at that level of power input, and witnessed a terrible tragedy at the plant. The electric mechanic assigned to us to wire up and run through the procedures had spent all his years dealing with electric power tooling. As he wired up the machine, he was smoking a cigarette and a small drop of ash fell on the hotplate. Without a thought he brushed off the ash with his hand. There was a terrific flash and the electrician was electrocuted on the spot. The power was switched off and he was pulled away. His overall was on fire and his body was charred to a cinder. We left the company very distressed at the accident.

We produced many special machines for Caterpillar Tractors from designs that we had submitted. We also designed equipment for Coventry Radiators, pressure vessels for Messers Mclaren and tooling for Morris Motors, Girling, Serk, Dunlop, Massey Ferguson Tractors and Cincinnati. We designed and made two special machines for Mclaren. They had to be designed for multi-heads to be fitted upside-down. The cast-iron casting needed very deep hole drilling and the swarf had been breaking many drills. So it was decided that if the multi-heads were driven upside down in the body of the machine and the component fixed to a top platform, then lowered onto the drills, the swarf would drop down rather than clog the drills. This turned out to be highly successful and drill breakage was reduced considerably.

We were called in to design and develop an automation device for a firm in Droitwich. Bars of steel 10 inches in diameter were being loaded on to a cut-off saw which cut them up to lengths of 8 inches, then transported them to a furnace for annealing, after which they were transported to the machine shop. We designed equipment that was capable of lifting the long bars from the steel stores, feeding the bar through the saw, stopping the saw at the correct stage and allowing the cut billet to fall on to a special device which carried the billet to the furnace for annealing and then on to the machine shop. The exercise was very successful, saved three operators and was able to operate 24 hours a day with no supervision.

A great friend of mine, Len Bowley of Crane Screw, phoned to see if we were interested in building ten special-purpose pointing machines. Apparently it was a job undertaken by their own tool room. Some of the machines were part-completed and not all the castings had been ordered. We could have the patterns. The company required an overall price to finish the part-completed machines plus complete building of the remainder. We had to offer a very low price indeed to take this work on but I owed Len a few favours and hoped this way we could square our debt.

We also produced a 12-foot-long machine to cut teeth in a rack, fully automatic and adjustable for all lengths of rack, with different pitches and different sizes of teeth, for Vickers of Newtown.

We had an order from Austin Motor Company to produce 50 fixtures to be used on a large automatic set-up. Every fixture had to be exactly identical so that the platerns on which the fixtures were fastened accurately arrived at a sequence of operations, and performed perfectly. There could be no variation from one fixture to the next so that the cutting tools were able to perform precisely at each stage. We delivered on time and Austin were well pleased.

Once I was called in to Austin's just as our works were to be closed for the July holiday. I called all the workers together and announced that Austin had placed an order with us for the complete tooling of the glove box of the Maxi model, on condition that we finished them in time for the Motor Show in October. This meant asking for volunteers to work through the two-week holiday. Many of the workers had paid deposits on their holiday bookings; some had even sent their luggage on in advance. In answer to my appeal every single one of the employees offered to forfeit their holidays and work through. It meant splitting the force into three sections of eight hours each and working through non-stop seven days a week. Everyone would be rewarded and holidays given after completion of the tooling. I worked on different shifts to keep up the morale. We finished the tools on time and were congratulated by Austin, who told us that as far as possible work would be found for us; we should not run short of orders.

One day a representative called and asked to look over the premises and have a list of our machines and their capacities. He was from Brockhurst Engineering in Gloucester; they were intending to build a factory to produce aircraft. He was to be the tool buyer and would be pleased to receive our quotation. We later received several orders and made every effort to please a new customer, paying particular attention to quality and accuracy. Our proud boast was that though we were not the cheapest, our products were always the best. We received an order from Brockhurst Engineering to produce 24 assembly frames into which radial engines could be lowered, the location plungers and clamps fixed in position and the rings swivelled, so that when released by the crane, the engine could be transported from one operation to the next and the frame revolved in order to present full access for the fitter. These frames carried the engines through the factory and when finished allowed the engine to be removed by the crane when the swivel rings were rotated. The only trouble with the contract was the delivery of the four swivel castors, supposed to be provided by Brockhurst Engineering. We had to deliver the units without castors and send a fitter down o Gloucester to fit them when available.

We made several large checking fixtures for Bristol Aeroplane Company, which meant the capacity of our machine shop was under stress. The bases of the fixtures needed precision turning up to a 7-foot diameter, and our jig borer, of 6-foot cubic capacity, was stretched to its limits. Handling large pieces of equipment required space to manoeuvre, difficult in a crowded workplace. Nevertheless we received many orders from Bristol plants.

We had advertised as machinists of fabricated structures and in reply we received orders from Coventry Lifting Trucks to produce checking jigs for the cross-slide and verticle bores in the framewok of fork-lift trucks' slides. These were quite a test of accuracy in machining the large pieces of assembly. We were congratulated by the Coventry firm, as they had been unable to find anybody to tackle these jobs in Coventry.

We were often called on to visit factories and suggest to them cheaper ways of producing their products, even though they had been looking at the problem for several years, without success. We would be given about two hours to suggest ways of improving their methods, estimate the cost of equipment required and the time required to recover the cost of the equipment.

We received an order from a Japanese firm to produce a sequence of machines to produce strips of imitation oak flooring in a zigzag pattern. Their suggested requirement was for six sets of the machines. We designed, developed and perfected the first set which was paid for and dispatched. In spite of repeated approaches, we had no further news of the other five sets we were hoping to produce. We believe they copied our products and produced them themselves.

We were doing a great deal of work for Rolls Royce. We had one of our engineers visit each plant in turn and enquire of all the departments if they had problems. He would then report to our designs department, leave details of the problem, collect designs and suggestions from previous weeks, report to inspection and collect any tools or equipment completed and deliver them to the plant on his next visit. Sometimes we did not receive the official order until long after the tools were being used on production and it was even longer before payment was made. Rolls Royce were always satisfied with our performance and we were placed second on their list of suppliers.

In about 1963 we became involved with Paintain Engineering of Northampton supplying special purpose machines and technical developments; I had made contact with them through my Engineering Industry Association (E.I.A.) and National Union of Manufacturing (N.U.M.) connections. We were asked to design a machine that would assemble plastic sockets and plugs that were used in the building of computers. Some sockets had two, three or four rows of assembled units; some units had to be vertical and some horizontal, and some had spaces in the rows. There were 24 different sockets. Each signal of a Yes impulse in the computer needed a horizontal unit and each signal of a No impulse needed a vertical unit. We designed a control plate for each separate socket. Each plate was made with different signals for horizontal and vertical stitchings and a control button when a space was needed in the rows of stitchings. The assembled units consisted of a clothes-peg-shaped plug with a spring inserted between the legs of the clothes-peg and a small shaped hole in the side to be locked on a small projection in the socket block. These operations were carried out by twelve operators and we had to design the machine to replace them. We produced a machine that operated the stitchings at two seconds per stitching and easily beat the output of the operators manually assembling the sockets. The two components required in the units were each fed by vibrators into an assembly ring. The clothes-peg was first fed into the ring which was then indexed round to accept the spring which had been compressed so that it could be inserted into the legs of the clothes-peg. The unit then fed into a plunger which performed the stitching. This plunger was controlled by a signal from the control plate which showed whether the unit was to be vertical or horizontal. The machine table would be organized by the control plate, as to how many units were needed in each row, when the end of the row was reached and indexed to the next row, until the assembly was complete.

We designed other equipment for Paintain Engineering which was never ordered such as the mating plug component assembly, a special machine for grading the strength of capacitors and a winding machine to produce coils for the electric motors used in the computers. They made a token payment towards the expenses incurred on design work.

The production manager at Paintain, George Thompson-Gordon, was a keen golfer; one day he suggested we fielded teams from our respective companies to play an annual golf match. We suggested the trophy be a wooden spoon, held by the loser and improved every year of being held. A closer rivalry developed, and we fielded four a side. We added a few extra conditions: among others, that the home team was to pay all expenses of the visitors, at every match a new ball would be provided to each player and any player losing his ball would be expected to buy a round of drinks at the 19th hole. This competition continued until the unfortunate death of George Thompson-Gordon.

We next entered the field of abrasive belt machinery. It was proved that an abrasive belt removed more material, was cooler and cheaper than normal grinding wheel techniques. For instance, you could hold in the hand a 2-inch-diameter drill against an abrasive belt and flat-bottom the drill point. The same operation could not be done with a grinding wheel without copious supplies of cooling water. The grains of the belt having further to travel arrived back at the cutting space much cooler than the grains of a grinding wheel, which only travelled the circumference of the grinding wheel. Abrasive belts were very much cheaper than grinding wheels.

We produced for Borg-Warner at Cardiff our largest automatic-controlled machine tool. It was a 24 station unit built each side of the square 30 feet long and included milling, drilling, taping and counter-boring two similar components. At the first station the operator was seated, and unloaded the finished components from the jig, replaced them with two sets of virgin components and set the machine in operation. The components not only passed through working positions but were tested by probes and automatic gap-gauges, all of which had fail-safe devices built in. If any of the probes or gauges failed to register, the machine was automatically stopped and a setter solved the cause by adjusting or replacing the faulty tools. King's Heath Automation Developments (K.H.E.A.D.), the electronic division of the company, completed all the wiring and control units of the machine. When the machine was finished at the works and the customer passed it as acceptable we had to dismantle and send it with two fitters to Cardiff to reassemble and run it through for acceptance by the company's production department. The building the fitters had to work in during severe winter snows and storms was only partly complete, the girderwork and roofing being intact, but the sides open to the elements.

One of K.H.E.'s most successful designs was of a brake shoe rolling machine. On one of many calls at the Ford Motor Company plant at Dagenham, for whom we manufactured many tools and on several occasions planned, designed and processed tooling, we were asked to design and produce a machine to create brake shoes from a straight T-section angle-iron.

Apparently Fords had been using a machine made in the United States which only produced 35 shoes an hour. Another machine from the States would cost £20,000 and delivery would be 18 months. A further drawback was that the time taken to change sizes was eight hours. First we produced figures showing that a machine designed by K.H.E.A.D. would make brake shoes at 1,000 an hour, could be manufactured for £15,000 and size could be changed in a quarter of an hour. Ford were impressed and ordered the machine. We built the machine in nine months, the only delay being the supply of the very large bearings required from the USA. On checking the costings, the machine was built for £13,000.

The machine was highly successful at Fords and we obtained a complimentary write-up in *Mechanical Engineering Magazine*. We patented the design, printed some leaflets and distributed them to companies engaged on brake shoe manufacture and worldwide agents for the supply of machine tools. We received orders from Dunlop, Girling and Pressed Steel as well as overseas enquiries from South Africa, New Zealand, Turkey and Korea. We had a cost saving on the patterns for all the castings required. We also received a stock of the large bearings from the USA for the possible needs of our customers to whom we suggested that they ordered extra bearings at the same time as placing their orders for the machine, as these were the most likely cause of breakdown. We had to obtain quotations for the machining of the main body of the machine, which was beyond the capacity of our machine plant. Moon Brothers were very cooperative in the early days and produced castings from our patterns and agreed to carry out the large machining for us. The payment of their charges produced a cash flow problem; as a small company we were being stretched beyond our financial resources.

From our contracts with Moon Brothers we were introduced to Barney Small from Chicago. Barney undertook to become our USA sales manager, obtained a provisional order from the States and indicated that other orders would follow. He asked to be appointed as a director of the company as well as USA sales manager, saying that this position would enable him to negotiate more successfully on our behalf. At a hurriedly called meeting of directors this proposal was carried.

12

Boat Trips Abroad

John Whorwood, Bobbie's husband, loved to come to Wroxham for the weekend and travel with us to the various stopping places we had discovered. We began to think of going further out to sea rather than just the short trips we made to Lowestoft and the Wash. John suggested that we think about taking *Freeleen* across the North Sea and have holidays in Belgium, the Netherlands and Denmark.

After a great deal of discussion we organized a holiday in the Netherlands the following year. I purchased tidal maps and maritime charts with full details of current drifts and sandbanks. We decided on a three-week holiday in Holland. We worked out the time to leave Yarmouth on the full tide, calculated tidal drift and possible wind deflection and charted a course to Rotterdam.

We loaded the boat and set off from Wroxham on a Saturday morning and sailed through the lock gates to Yarmouth harbour. The weather report was not good so we moored in the Yarmouth harbour overnight. We set off on full tide at 6 a.m. the next morning. We had a basket of oranges with us; it was amazing what a good navigational aid orange peel proved to be. Every half-hour somebody ate an orange and dropped the peel in the wake. The peel was visible well past the fading of the wake and we were able to check our tidal drift. It was just out of range before the next orange was due.

We made good time and the first land sighted turned out to be the Hague, recognizable from the charts showing skyline features. We were only about two miles north of the course we had set and since we had been out of sight of land for 14 hours I suppose that was not bad. We adjusted course and steered for Rotterdam harbour, where we moored at about 8.30 p.m.

At about 10.00 a.m. next day we were asked by the harbour master to vacate the harbour as a fishing trawler had captured a live sea mine in its nets and was slowly approaching. Everybody was to vacate the area whilst the army specialists defused the mine. We explained that we could not move – our batteries were flat and would not be ready until the evening. The harbour was cleared of all other boats and all the neighbouring houses cleared of occupants, while barriers were erected. The fishing vessel moved slowly into the dock, and the fishermen were evicted. The only people allowed in the area were the army specialists and ourselves. We were within 100 yards of the trawler and we could clearly see the mine tied up in the nets and suspended from the yardarm. It took about two hours to defuse the mine and then everything returned to normal.

Later we visited the Schedam Yacht Club and introduced ourselves. We were treated royally and particularly admired for having crossed the North Sea, which was very shallow for several miles off this part of the coast. If the sea was only slightly choppy the waves bounced on the sea bottom and surfaced with double strength, so the yachtsmen of Holland did not venture out of sight of the shore.

Leaving Rotterdam we sailed down the Rhine valley towards Amsterdam. The river crossed a good many lakes en route, always populated with numerous sailing boats. At one point we had dozens of children trying to hang onto the towing dinghy for a ride as we passed by. I was afraid of them being injured by the propeller so speeded up to avoid their clutches. Then I noticed a sailing boat ahead suddenly heel over and change direction. I closed the throttle and slowed right down – just as well because a wire rope was tightly strung across the river, used to pull a ferry boat across the river. If we had not stopped, the superstructure of the boat would have been sliced off.

On reaching Amsterdam we moored in one of the canals close to the city centre, intending to stay there for several days.

In Amsterdam I had difficulties posting some cards home. I had enquired of some passer-by where to post letters and they seemed to point to the other side of the street. Eventually, having crossed and walked fruitlessly up and down, I enquired again. Again they seemed to point across the street. After about four crossings and having searched the street for a postbox, I finally asked someone how to post my cards. He led me to the centre of the road, and when a tram stopped, showed me the postbox fastened to its side. My previous informants must all have pointed to a passing tram.

We stayed in Amsterdam for several nights and toured the highways and canals, for there was plenty to see. We saw the famous barrel organ with tame monkeys climbing about and assistants with collecting boxes circulating in the crowd. At one of our evening meals we celebrated David's half-birthday. When the staff heard our celebrations we were served with a birthday cake and each of us with a glass of brandy.

We left Amsterdam and sailed the boat to The Hague. On arrival we could not find anywhere to moor, but finally found a stretch of lawn in front of a magnificent mansion of a house. We tied up and I went to find the owner. The butler arrived at the door and soon after the owner, a real aristocratic gentleman, came and asked what I wanted and whence we had travelled. When I said England, he said, 'You can moor anywhere in Holland for two nights free, but on the third night I will charge you.' He emphasized the charge would be exorbitant. He told the butler to look after his English friends. We were allowed deckchairs to sit on the lawn, our water tank was filled and the cook brought us many dishes of food. When we walked out of the grounds into the city of Hague we passed through massive iron gates at the entrance. We enjoyed our stay at The Hague, looking over the many museums, art galleries, and government buildings and admiring the skill of the Dutch masters. But we made sure we left after our two nights' stay.

We then returned inland and crossed the Zuider Zee, after a visit to Harlem to see the tulips. We also visited Immagen before returning to England. We walked around the docks there and saw the fishing company unloading fish; the sorting and processing all done with mechanical robots and packaging machinery.

We waited for weather forecasts and arranged to set off at high tide the next morning at 4.00 a.m. I was first awake, cast off, started the engines and took the helm, setting a course due west. The rest of the crew stirred about four hours later and prepared breakfast. John took over the helm to give me a break. We sailed throughout the day, out of sight of land for some 16 hours, steering due west the whole time.

Soon it began to get dark and we were still out of sight of land. John set to with maps and compasses and proposed we set a course for Southwold. He gave me the readings on a light in the distance, which he said was the harbour light at the entrance to the estuary, on the port side of the channel. Keeping the light on the port side and sailing in complete darkness we suddenly ran aground on the beach at Southwold. We opened the forward hatch and asked David to climb up and jump off as far forward as he could. The poor lad was half-asleep but did as he was told and found himself on the beach with a crowd round him. He asked them, 'Am I in heaven?'

The tide and sea-swell swung the boat round broadside to the waves. Everything on board was taking a real hammering as the boat was lifted by each wave and thundered back onto the beach.

The harbour master came to see us and suggested that we remove everything possible off the boat to prevent further damage. The harbour light that John had directed me toward was the one on the top of the town hall; the harbour light we should have used was 200 yards further south.

We removed everything possible from the boat and Eileen sat with it all on the sea wall. By now it was pouring with rain and she sat in the middle of about 60 yards of personal luggage: radio, cooking stove, television set, dinghy, outboard motors, golf clubs, kettles and cooking tackle, rescue equipment, life-raft and all the instruments we had been able to dismantle – an image I will always remember.

The harbour master registered us all in one of the seafront hotels as 'shipwrecked mariners'. He said that at full tide, at about 6.00 a.m., he would bring another boat round and try to tow *Freeleen* off the beach. Meanwhile he loaded all our belongings and tackle into his van and drove off to store them in his lock-up building.

I rose at 6.00 a.m., dressed and went to the beach just as the vessel arrived to try and drag our boat off the shore. A line was passed aboard and a tow rope fixed. The rope broke and a strong hauser took its place. The offshore vessel really tried to move *Freeleen* but failed to make any impression. All the seamen decided that it would need at least two boats, but I suggested that we fastened the tow line to the bow of the boat and waded in to help push out the bow. I set an example and pushed the bow with all my might. Suddenly the tow rope held and the boat made its first move; with one more shove the *Freeleen* moved off the shore and was towed to safety. I like to believe that I pushed twelve-ton *Freeleen* single-handedly off the beach.

The next day we spent fixing all fittings and equipment back in place.

The harbour master and the crew of the towing vessel applied to my insurers for salvage money. I supported their claim, for without their help *Freeleen* would have broken up on the seashore. This also helped in obtaining a caravan cheaply. We used the caravan to stay in when we visited the area.

Pat had a friend at Evesham boat yard named Andy Sankey-Smith, and was seeing a lot of him over weekends. She asked if he could join us on boat trips and we agreed. About this time we were considering a sea trip to France, mooring in Paris and seeing the sights of the city. George Pielow of Francis Davies Lodge had heard of our experiences in Holland and expressed a wish to join us on our next cruise.

So we organized a crew meeting at Southam Road to finalize plans: what times suited everybody, what time to start, course to set, details of food required, fuel required, approximate costs involved, the maps we would need and arrangements to be made.

We decided to take a trip to Folkestone and find a possible mooring before the crossing to France. We reached Folkestone at high tide and moored against the sea wall. The locals told us that the tide receded from the wall and we would be left high and dry. We returned to the boat and found the batteries had run flat and there was not enough power to start the engine. So we removed the batteries, organized their recharge and managed to get a mooring in the tideway. We used the dinghy to tow the boat to the mooring and return to the shore.

By now George had had enough, so making some excuse he took a train back to Birmingham. He never joined us on our French trip.

After this episode we decided not to use Folkestone for an overnight stay but steer straight for Ramsgate and make the channel crossing from there. Andy joined us for the trip and we obtained a petrol-driven battery-charging unit.

We set off early one Saturday morning with the prospect of a three-week holiday, with one week to reach Paris, one week moored near the Place de la Concorde and one week for the return trip. In the first attempt at the Channel crossing the cooling water-pump seized up. We had to call in at Dover for replacement hose fittings, then set off for Boulogne, intending to make for Le Havre and proceed down the Seine. But after calling into Boulogne we were issued with a blue entry passport so we decided to make for Dieppe and join the Seine nearer to Paris. After a night's sleep we sailed to Dieppe and stayed in a small village along the river. We stopped overnight, filled up the craft with diesel and drinking water on board and set off to Paris. On the way we passed a small dinghy fitted with a small outboard engine that was in trouble with weeds clogging the propeller. They had crossed the Channel and were very disappointed that they would be unable to reach Paris. So we arranged to tow them until we reached the river Seine, about two days' sailing away. We went through several locks and had to tip the lock-keeper on every occasion. We reached the Seine, said goodbye to our friends and progressed towards Paris, just one day behind schedule.

On Sunday morning at about 11.00 a.m. we were sailing down the Seine in gorgeous weather, all of us drinking sherry on the poop deck, with David at the helm proceeding quietly downstream. Suddenly there was a loud bang and the boat stopped. We looked to see that the drive plate connecting the engine to the propeller shaft was twisted off. Something had got wedged between the 'A' bracket and the propeller. So stripping off to a bathing costume I went over the side to examine the damage and found a large piece of timber wedged in the housing. With help from on board I was able to set free the propeller and extract the piece of timber. We had to struggle to realign the engine, and by cannibalizing all the nuts and bolts off the toilet we managed to refasten the drive plate and make way again.

On arriving at the mooring reserved on the Seine near the Place de la Concorde we managed to find an engineer who offered to make a new drive plate and provide a new set of nuts and bolts. It cost us about £80, the equivalent of one person's travel allowance. (In those days we were restricted to the amount of money we were allowed to take abroad.)

We spent a week moored in Paris, but could only stay on the boat in the evenings when the pleasure steamers had finished for the day, because when they were working the wake of the steamers rocked *Freeleen* like crazy.

We toured the city of Paris: the museums, the art galleries, Montmartre, the Left Bank and the Eiffel Tower. We had several enjoyable meals and every other night we went to a night club and saw a lot of Paris nightlife. After a week we arranged our departure, and decided to take the route to Calais, giving us a shorter Channel crossing. We passed through many magnificent locks, some about 100 feet high and large enough to take six barges. We arrived at one of the largest locks on the journey to find a large crowd of onlookers and were about to moor up and wait for a working barge to arrive, when the lights changed and signalled us to enter. The lock was about 300 feet long and about 60 feet wide, and the gates closed before we could fasten to the side. The lock-keeper then decided to open the sluices in the diagonally opposite corners, causing a massive whirlpool. The boat was sent in a huge circle, with all of us frantically fending the boat off the walls of the lock as we were spun round at a fantastic speed. The dinghy broke free of the painter and went off on a spin all on its own. Just as we were mastering the conditions the lock-keeper switched the incoming jets to the opposite corners and after a tremendous turbulence reversed the direction of the whirlpool. The crowd of watchers thought our plight hilarious and cheered our discomfort with great glee. I could cheerfully have strangled that lock-keeper with my bare hands. We stayed in the lock some time to get everything shipshape again before I paid my lock fee.

When we finally arrived at Calais we had further problems. The final lock keeper would not let us enter Calais harbour on the blue passport. It had to be green. Apparently the blue one issued meant that we had to return through Boulogne. To get the visa changed we had to find the harbour master, who was not on duty until 11.30 a.m. while the main sea lock was only open until 12.30. So I had to run about two miles to reach the harbour master's office, get the visa changed, pay the fee, return to the boat, clear details with the lock-keeper, clear the lock and get the boat back and through the main lock in the half-hour before the lock gates closed until the next tide. I just about managed this and just got through the main lock gates before they closed. We tied up to the sea wall and set about getting *Freeleen* seaworthy. Suddenly we were showered with over-ripe fruit squashing all around us. Finally, after a great deal of shouting, the tradesman above realized someone was below the wall and ceased discarding his missiles.

Finally we set off as the tide was receding rapidly. The outlook was very misty and visibility was down to about 30 yards. We set a course to miss the dreaded Dogger Bank. Eileen was posted as forward lookout. The only buoy she saw was the North Dogger Bank which meant we had crossed the sandbank on a falling tide. The danger of the bank is that if ever a craft becomes stranded the bow and the stern become fixed and the rising tide then washes away the support under the keel and breaks the spine of the boat. Anyway we made Ramsgate and we were all glad to be back on English soil.

After an overnight stay, we sailed for Southword, tied up

at the sea wall and the girls disembarked. Andy and I would return *Freeleen* by sea to Wroxham. I took the helm and suddenly noticed a sign on the dockside warning of underwater obstacles. Too late, we bashed into them and the sudden lurch jerked me forward and smashed my glasses into my eyes. Andy took the helm back to the dockside. Blood gushing everywhere, I was helped off the boat and some kind fellow led me to his car to take me to Norwich hospital. With his lights on, horn blowing and swerving from side to side at breakneck speed we reached casualty. I do not remember much else for I passed out. I was in hospital for two nights. Eileen and Bobbie stayed on the boat until I was released by the hospital and went with them from there back home. There had been lots of glass in my eye and the surgeon said that three small pieces remained and would work themselves out. They never did and as far as I know they are still in there.

13

My Masonic Experiences

I was initiated into my father's lodge, Francis Davies, on 27th January 1947 and from the next meeting in February was invited to act as Steward in the Lodge. I was never out of the office until I resigned from the Lodge as Chaplain in 1972.

In December 1948, at the Ladies' Night meeting, one of the young masons sang the Ladies' Song and fell ill, collapsed and died in the ambulance on the way to hospital. He left a wife, daughter and son.

A member of the Lodge, on enquiring of their circumstances, reported back to the Lodge and immediate arrangements were made to offer the wife a situation and both the children were enrolled in the Masonic Girls and Masonic Boys Schools. The Lodge attended the schools every other year. We sent the children gifts on their birthdays and Christmas. They wrote back to us as uncle masons. After their education the girl became matron at a London hospital and the boy became a solicitor and formed his own company, also in London.

There was a further incident which occurred during my Masonic involvement. One of the elder masons died and his wife was interviewed and we were told that she was penniless, unable to pay the rent and lived very frugally. She was admitted to the Masonic Old Peoples Home and was well provided for. The Grand Master of Worcestershire paid her a visit and reported to us on one of his visits that the lady had asked him to express her gratitude. She was 51 years old on entering the home, has been waited on hand and foot ever sine, is now 102 years old and has doubled her life span.

I joined the Lodge of Instruction and three years later became Assistant Preceptor to W Br Wright and W Br Toy and in 1950 succeeded as Preceptor of the Lodge of Instruction. I became a Founder Member of Weatheroak Lodge in 1952. The Weatheroak officers joined the Francis Davies Lodge of Instruction. In 1972 because of a change of circumstances I had to resign from all Masonic Lodges and move to North Wales.

In 1960 I joined the Shenstonian Lodge on the basis of entry as my son was now a scholar at Solihull Public School. (Shenstonian Lodge was formed by the masters and parents of pupils at the school and you had to be one or the other to join the lodge.) Later I became Assistant Preceptor to the Lodge of Instruction there so there were times in my career when I was involved in the course of a single week rehearsing all the degrees in Masonry. In 1972 again I had to retire.

14

Ruin

It seemed our humble company had expanded into a very large combine. All too soon we were heavily committed to manufacturing costs. Bearings had to be paid for with orders and large materials costs loomed up. Without financial help we were going to struggle to cover basic costs.

Moon Brothers helped and arranged to pay for the first machine required by the USA in exchange for a transfer of the franchise for the supply of brake shoe rolling machines. At this stage they had all our patterns and castings required for all our orders but held up machining pending settlements of outstanding accounts.

We tried to obtain progress payment for the financing of early expenditure. Pressed Steel of Coventry were reluctant to pass a progress payment to Moon Brothers for the machining costs. Moon Brothers pressed for the rights of manufacture of brake shoe rolling machines from us.

Suddenly the sky fell on us. Our designs and manufacture of tools for Rolls Royce had also advanced into a critical cash flow problem. Our continuous efforts to supply Rolls Royce with designs and tooling had resulted in their owing £68,000 to us. We had produced tools for Rolls Royce in advance of payment because of the pressure on us to complete tooling for the RB211.

Edward Heath, the then prime minister, decided in order to

discredit the contract made by Labour MP Anthony Wedgewood Benn for the supply of RB211 engines to the USA, to place the Rolls Royce company in liquidation and negotiate a new deal. This was purely a political manoeuvre, for even today Rolls Royce is still a viable company. In my opinion this was a very damaging option. Rolls Royce represented the epitome of precision engineering. (This was demonstrated when America offered to produce Rolls Royce Merlin engines during the war, but were unable to achieve the high performance that Rolls Royce produced and asked the British company to investigate. Rolls Royce engineers found that the Americans had widened the tolerances specified on the drawings, to ease manufacture. As soon as the tolerances were restored the results compared with the British firm's performance).

All our overseas orders were cancelled and we were faced with an insurmountable problem. The Midland Bank refused to advance payment of our wage bill. Within one week the collapse of our company was inevitable. After 24 years in business and through no fault of mine we were finished.

The final week had started with a phone call to the bank asking them to assist in providing payment of our wages by Friday. I was told to find the cover before calling and to discount anything at all from Rolls Royce. I spent a frantic week phoning. Cheques from Sankeys, Ford and Rubery Owen were all supposed to be in the computer and would arrive in due course. I managed to collect a few hundreds in small amounts, insufficient for our needs. I really thought payments for our wages were feasible. We had reduced our overdraft from £26,000 to £14,000 and I thought that since the company was worth that once there should have been an amount of slack that could be taken up.

I arrived at the Midland Bank at 10.00 a.m. The bank immediately appointed a receiver as their representative and he was sitting in my chair on my return.

I then had to address the full complement of the employees, some that had been with me from the start of amalgamation of the companies. Wages and redundancies would be settled by the receiver. Most of my employees obtained jobs that same afternoon. The standard of work produced by my company was well known and my employees were in great demand, some even obtained jobs paying higher wages and some obtained jobs nearer home. Because I was the principal shareholder I had no redundancy and had to stay with the company until all work in progress was completed and all accounts cleared. I was just paid expenses. This lasted a full month before the auction sales took place.

The value of the company's machine tools at book value, reduced by annual depreciation to a total of £70,000, and originally costing twice that figure, raised a total of £20,000 under the hammer. Steel and materials of value £50,000 were sold for under £10,000. Vehicles, office furniture, fixtures and fittings were practically given away.

After being 24 years in business and having done nothing wrong I was reduced to penury.

My five-bedroomed house, my Jaguar, my wife's and daughters' cars, my boat-hire business and my caravan sites were all sold. The full collateral security to the banks for all subsidiary companies were paid in full. The money outstanding in my loan account with the company of £8,000 had to be written off. This was wages I had not drawn and money I had loaned the firm from time to time. We moved to a rented two-roomed flat in Yardley when all our assets were disposed of. We were destitute. I had been worth £500,000 at the start of our troubles and finished with the clothes I stood up in.

The crowning humiliation was my first visit to the local employment office. On previous occasions the manager had rung me in person to ask if I could find employment for various people; I obliged on every occasion, fitting them in somewhere in the organization. I phoned to ask if he would see me and he replied that he was too busy, so I had to join the queue. I filled in the form and waited in the human cauldron. Some slip of a girl just from school called out, 'Shelley, you have filled your form out wrong.' I made the correction, picked up my dole money and walked out.

I walked aimlessly for about six hours. I know now why in such circumstances failed businessmen commit suicide. I wallowed in misery for days.

Meanwhile my wife and children set about organizing our future. Eileen said to me, 'No matter if we have to live in a tent in a field, so long as we stay together.' This did more than anything to help me put all the problems on one side and consider the best way forward.

Of everything I owned only *Freeleen*, registered in Eileen's name, and the caravan site in North Wales, in Mother's name, survived. We moved the boat to Southport on the River Severn. We had many family trips to fish off the boat and greatly enjoyed the weekends we spent there. When the boat was finally sold it paid the initial deposit on our last house in North Wales.

The bank had the deeds of the house at Southam Road, so that had to be sold as soon as possible. All the house contents were disposed of by Eileen, the house was sold and all the proceeds went to the Midland Bank.

I sent a telegram to Barney Small explaining the situation. It happened that Barney had one of the Elliot brothers, the plier manufacturers, with him at the time, who said that the company in Cannock were looking for a production manager. This started another chapter in my career.

15

North Wales and Retirement

I applied for the job at the Elliot Plier Company and was accepted. It was a lower salary than I had been getting, but my expenses were much lower.

For a time I travelled back and forth from Yardley to Cannock, and settled in to a new environment. I found it difficult to take orders and not be fully responsible for everything that happened. I made a complete study of the products produced and sent a report to the managing director who had interviewed me and confirmed my appointment. One of the problems seemed to be lack of incentive of the workforce, so I developed a simple formula, dividing work produced by hours taken. It was a long process to convince the operators that the change would benefit them. Finally when the bonus calculations were worked out production increased and the workforce accepted the advantages in increased pay. Another idea I introduced was periods of music while you work. I had a great deal of opposition from management on this, so I started the scheme of using my own money to pay for the initial trial period. Another thing that I pressed for was better ventilation and after being asked to investigate costs suddenly found that equipment had been ordered and installation planned.

Soon after I had settled in at Cannock my Aunt Vin passed away and Mother was left on her own at Glan-y-Mor Towyn.

Eileen decided that she would go to Wales and look after Mother. We gave up the flat at Yardley and I lodged with my daughter Pat and her husband Michael for a time. Later on, when Pat was expecting a baby, I found digs in Cannock and travelled up to Wales every Friday night and back to Cannock for Monday morning. The digs I had found in Cannock were comfortable but the landlady was a terrible cook. It was a good job I had a good midday meal at the work's canteen and in Wales at the weekend.

I had been a country member of Abergele Golf Club for eight years, so I was also able to get a game of golf at weekends. One Sunday I played with John Lowe and told him how much I would appreciate a job in North Wales. He said he had seen an advertisement asking for engineers in North Wales to apply for a job at the Engineering Training Board at Cardiff. I applied for the job and was accepted. If I was prepared to pay a lump sum I could join the pension scheme, which proved of considerable benefit later on. At last something seemed to have gone right for me. Again I had to accept a lower wage but expenses were paid. For a time I ran my own car until a vehicle was supplied by the Board. My district spread from Chester in the east to the Isle of Anglesey and the Lleyn peninsula in the west down to Aberystwyth on the west coast to Builth Wells in Abergavenny in the south and to the borders of Hereford in the south-east. I had 250 firms on my patch and I tried to visit one at least once every year. I was able to make many suggestions to improve the quality and improve the output at many of the companies in my area. One firm I visited had orders to produce large reels for paper mills. The reels were turned out of 10-inch diameter steel billets about 12 inches long. They were produced on two lathes in line and every time a new block was required to be set up in any one lathe the other carried on working until it too had to have another block set up. This meant that the two milling machinists on the other side of the gangway had to cease work to allow the donkey engine to remove the finished reel from the lathe; reverse, and return with a new block to be set up. This procedure had to be repeated for the second lathe before the milling machines could resume work. I suggested that the machine layout be altered so that the two lathes be set up side by side, head to tail, and that they erect a gibbet with a swinging gantry between the lathes so that either lathe could be loaded independently. The two milling machines could then be moved into the space left by one of the lathes and no time would be lost in the change-over. The firm acted on my suggestions; on my next visit I was thanked for my advice which had improved production by a considerable amount and reduced waiting time.

I suggested savings in another firm which was assembling spindles with multiple components, fitted on and fastened with two nuts, one at each end. The operators were assembling the parts and struggled with two spanners to tighten the nuts. I suggested a socket be fastened to the bench so that one nut could be located and the components collected from trays fitted to a semicircular rack so that the operator could collect the components in correct rotation, fix them on the spindle, add the second nut and with one spanner tighten the assembly. This change proved highly successful.

I also had to deliver lectures to sixth-formers at various schools to convince them that engineering was a highly valuable profession and extol the virtues of an engineering apprenticeship. I used to start the talks by going through the improvements in our lives brought about by engineering skills. The way we used to travel from A to B was by foot or on horseback. Now engineering had developed transport by cycles, cars, trains, aircraft, and supersonic flight – even rockets to the moon. In our daily lives the development of radio, television, compact discs, mobile telephones and advanced sound reproduction, had all been the work of engineers. What of the future? I foresaw the possibility of every house having a small windmill on its roof, swivelling to the direction of the wind, energy being transmitted to generators which would charge a collection of batteries fitted into the roof space which would supply each house with enough electricity for cooking, heating, cleaning, hot water and all daily needs. We need only look at the capacity of batteries used to power space rockets and hearing aids to realise the potential of a series of batteries. In the years ahead you would be able to speak to the wall and your words would be transmitted to the other side of the world, translated into any language. You would be able to fax pictures anywhere in the world.

I retired from the Training Board on my 65th birthday. I had a good send-off from Cardiff and afterwards worked part-time for Mid- and North Wales Training Association. This lasted about one year. Then I concentrated on running Avondale Camp. By this time Mother was living with us at Abergele and the camp needed a great deal of work to enable us to register with the Welsh Holiday Council. I managed the Avondale Camp until 1991 and sold it just before the Towyn floods.

After the sale of the campsite I suppose we vegetated a little in our backwater, just making occasional trips to Pat and to David to see our grandchildren. All the children knew of the fortune-teller's prediction that Eileen would live to be 75, and as her 75th birthday drew near, Pat began to organize a massive celebration party. All our friends from London, Birmingham and Bristol were invited. Eileen's 75th birthday was on 30th August, Bank Holiday Monday 1993.

Pat arranged a private plane to fly us down from Manchester to Basingstoke, without Eileeen knowing anything about it. It was to be a complete surprise. The pilot told Pat that if the conditions were good he would allow Eileen to handle the controls for a short time. I had to promise that

Eileen would know nothing of the arrangements until the last moment.

On the preceding Thursday, my usual day for golf, I told Eileen that because of it being Open Week at the club I could not play at Abergele and suggested that I play at Denbigh instead. But really I drove to Manchester Airport to check the flight details and meet the pilot. I called at Denbigh Golf Club on my return, had a pint of beer and returned home. I told Eileen that Pat had asked a friend of hers who lived near Manchester Airport to drive us to Pat's house on Monday. I explained that the friend lived close to the airport, so I could park there, but we must be there by 8.00 a.m.

We prepared everything on Sunday night, loaded up the car and backed it into the garage so that we could drive straight out. When everything was ready we went to bed, I kissed Eileen and she went to sleep straight away, breathing deeply and evenly. I put out the light and went to sleep. At about 3.00 a.m. I was awakened by Eileen screaming. I put the light on and said, 'You have got cramp. Sit on the side of the bed and I will get a cold compress.' Whilst in the bathroom I heard a loud thud – Eileen had fallen to the floor. I placed a pillow under her head and covered her with a blanket and asked if she wanted me to get anything. She tried to speak but just moved her mouth, not making a sound. I guessed straight away that she was suffering a stroke. I rang the doctor immediately and he arrived within ten minutes, diagnosed a massive stroke, rang for an ambulance and reserved a bed at the hospital. The ambulance arrived within minutes; I just put on trousers and coat over my pyjamas, phoned Pat to tell her the sad news and drove off to the hospital.

Bobbie attended the bedside every morning from 6.00 to 9.00 a.m. and I was there from 9.00 a.m. to 9.00 p.m. every day. During the whole time we were there she never gave any indication of recognition or response until she finally passed away on Tuesday, 28th September at 4.30 p.m. All the time I was with her I squeezed her little finger, because we used to say, if I loved her and could not say so, to squeeze her little finger. So if ever she felt any response at all she knew I loved her.

We all believe that, in effect she died on her 75th birthday.

Later Bobbie and I attended a meeting with a medium who described Eileen exactly and said that she had stood by Bobbie when she visited the chapel of rest. She said that she had spoiled me rotten during her life. I agreed.

From that time I realized that my own time was near and that I had nearly run my life's course. I looked forward to joining my sweetheart and to seeing again those two brown eyes smiling down at me.